SELF MADE

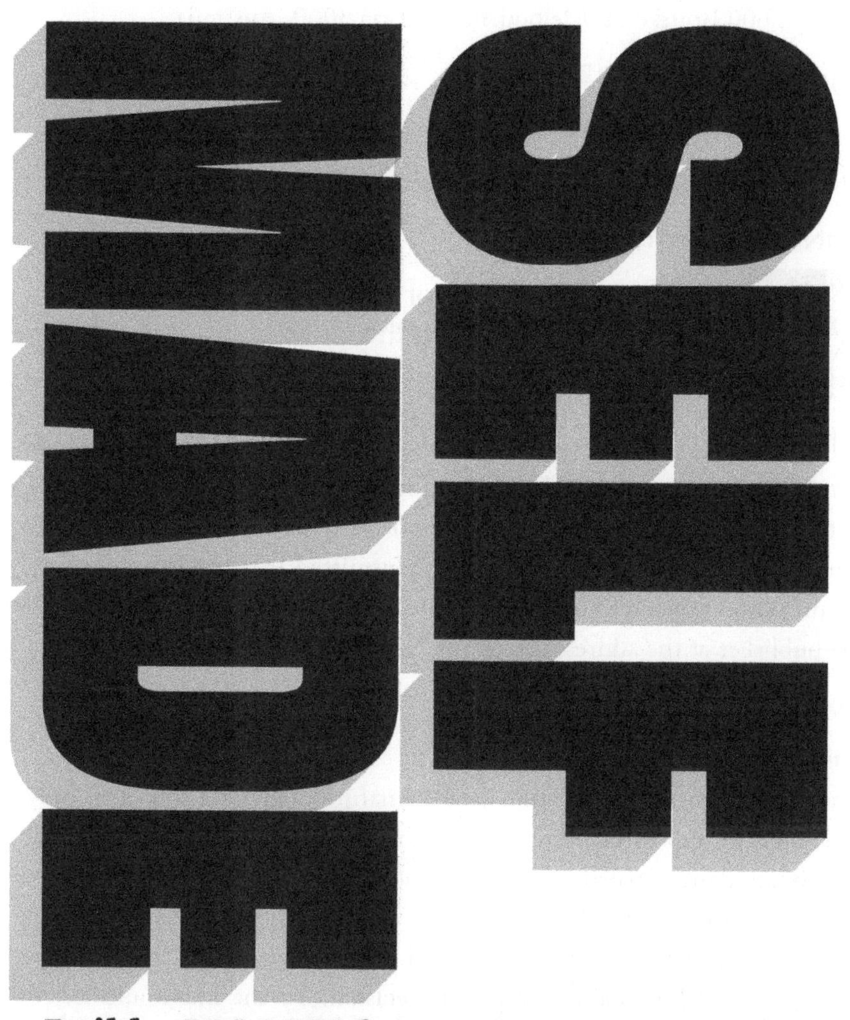

Build a BIG LIFE from a SMALL BUSINESS

OLIVIA CARR

Founder of Shhh Silk

WILEY

First published in 2024 by John Wiley & Sons Australia, Ltd
Level 4, 600 Bourke St, Melbourne Victoria 3000, Australia

Typeset in Bembo Std 12/16pt

ISBN: 978-1-394-19454-4

A catalogue record for this book is available from the National Library of Australia

Cover design by Wiley

Disclaimer

The material in this publication is of the nature of general comment only, and does not represent professional advice. It is not intended to provide specific guidance for particular circumstances and it should not be relied on as the basis for any decision to take action or not take action on any matter which it covers. Readers should obtain professional advice where appropriate, before making any such decision. To the maximum extent permitted by law, the author and publisher disclaim all responsibility and liability directly or indirectly sustained by taking or not taking action based on the information in this publication. The information provided in this book is not intended to be a substitute for professional medical advice, diagnosis, or treatment. If you are experiencing mental health issues or concerns, it is strongly recommended that you seek the advice of a qualified mental health professional. It is also recommended that you do not delay in seeking professional help or support if you are suffering from mental health issues. If you are experiencing a mental health emergency, it is recommended that you call emergency services or go to your nearest hospital emergency department immediately.

SKY56A82D4A-10B4-455E-B27B-D3EDD196C0F2_112323

For my two children, Georgia and Hudson.

Thank you for being my biggest cheerleaders and my greatest teachers. For allowing me to experience unconditional love. As you travel through life, remember, just like your childhood, the path ahead won't always be clear or without obstacles. But you have everything within you already to navigate every challenge or hardship you face. You also have all of the love inside you that you will ever need. So whenever you feel lost, return within.

Love always and forever, Mum xo

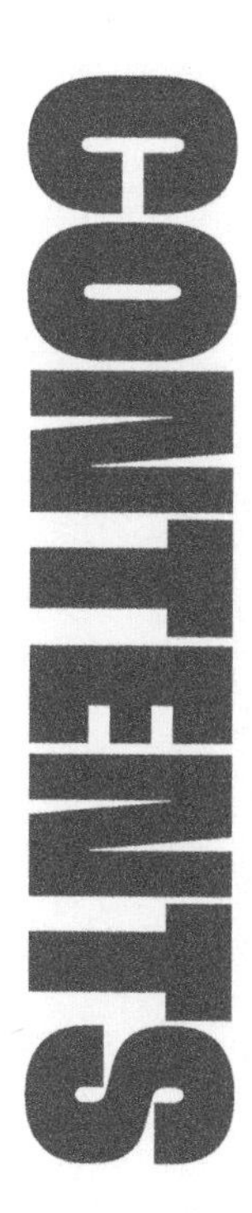
CONTENTS

INTRODUCTION: A SELF-MADE JOURNEY

If you've picked up this book, you may be curious what the title means? Perhaps you, yourself, are looking to become self-made, or maybe you were intrigued by what makes me, the author of this book, self-made.

Let me start by sharing the Oxford English Dictionary definition of self-made:

made by oneself

having become successful or rich by one's own efforts

Throughout this book you will discover what it is to be self-made, and how you, too, can become your own version of self-made. But before you read on, I want to say straight up that being self-made isn't just about a measure of financial success, and becoming self-made doesn't mean you have to aspire to having more than seven digits in your bank account. Heck, it doesn't even mean you have to have six! (Spoiler: it is possible though, irrespective of your current financial situation.)

Who am I?

First, let me introduce myself. I am Olivia Carr—mother, founder, philanthropist, mentor, keynote speaker, community builder, author and a self-made woman.

In this book, I share with you all of the tips, the lessons, the secrets, the stories and the tools that I have used to help me overcome hardship, adversity, financial struggle, relationship breakdowns, mental health challenges, and personal and professional setbacks and then go on to achieve my version of success and to become self-made.

Most traditional business books often start by showcasing the author's impressive credentials—their prestigious university degrees and their list of accomplishments. But not all successful people have followed this path, and I certainly have not had a typical path to success.

While I don't hold any university qualifications, I have certainly earned a master's degree in life experience, and that is something that cannot be taught inside a university lecture hall. Both my diverse life experience and strong mindset are what have allowed me to go from being in over $100 000 in debt in my 20s to building and growing a multi-million-dollar global brand. I started my business Shhh Silk in my spare room in 2015, and our products have become loved and adored by customers, retail outlets, hotels and A-list celebrities worldwide.

I wrote this book to not only serve as your very own personal guide to business success, but to help you achieve greater mental strength and, in turn, greater overall success in your life.

This book is full of practical, honest and actionable steps you can take right now to become self-made, no matter your current life or financial situation. How do I know this? Because I've been there. I have experienced my own version of rock bottom. And in this book, I share with you what those moments have taught me about mental strength, resilience, determination and tenacity. Learning to master these traits has helped me climb my way back up, and achieve more success and personal growth than I ever dreamt possible. This was my driving force for writing this book: to help you achieve more success and personal growth than you have ever dreamt was possible.

Finding strength from within

My biggest rock-bottom moment in life was when I was facing serious financial trouble. The lowest point was when I found myself standing in the Melbourne Magistrates' Court facing potential prison time for six years of unpaid CityLink fines, over 200 enforcement warrants, as well as multiple maxed-out credit cards, putting me at just over $100 000 in debt in my 20s.

How was this possible at such a young age? The cost of raising a child as a young, single mother, and falling into the trap of living beyond my means had caught up with me. I didn't know how to work my way out of it, and I felt like I would never get ahead. My financial problems felt too big and too hard to handle. I didn't know where to start to begin to turn my life around, or how I would ever be able to get ahead. The thought of one day owning my own home or building a successful business seemed like impossible dreams.

I eventually did turn my life around, and I share all of these lessons with you in this book so that you have the insights and strategies that I wish I had sooner when I was going through the very real struggles of financial pressure. We'll go through personal finance and professional cashflow lessons to help you turn your personal financial position or your business cash flow position around a lot sooner than I did.

Among all of the lessons and tips in this book, I also share moments of my personal story, which is one of perseverance, resilience, mental strength and determination. It's a story of rising from the depths of despair to build a successful business from scratch as a single mother, not once, but twice. It's through sharing my story with you that I hope to empower you with the tools that you may need to turn your life around, develop your self-belief to start your own business, grow your current business, or simply experience more personal growth and learn how to become self-made.

Self-made doesn't happen overnight

Becoming self-made was not an overnight process for me. It took me 14 years of hard work, sacrifice and commitment to finally clear all of my debt, and a further five years to teach myself how to reshape my mental relationship with money, how to manage money and how to respect money.

For all the mummas (or mummas-to-be) reading this, balancing the demands of parenthood with the constant needs of entrepreneurship is a continual challenge. There are many days, still, when I feel so overwhelmed and on the brink of giving up. I have learnt through my experiences what it takes to keep going and growing in the face of adversity.

Your purpose needs to be bigger than your problems. You need to understand what drives you, and we'll go through this process together. For me, it's my desire to create personal wealth and stability for myself; to be able to have the time and money to focus on my overall mental, physical and personal development; to be able to contribute to the community and pay it forward regularly; and to continue to make myself proud.

What you'll find in this book

Self-Made is your step-by-step guide to overcoming adversity and achieving success.

Throughout the pages of *Self-Made*, I share insights, strategies and advice that I believe are crucial for success: from your initial decision to start your own business, to the challenges of growing and scaling it. We'll also work on cultivating a self-made mindset, and tap into your inner strength and resilience to create the life you desire, regardless of your current obstacles. Throughout the chapters of this book, you will tap into a wealth of knowledge about building and growing your business—knowledge that I wish I had access to when I began my entrepreneurial journey. This book is like having a mentor in your corner every step of the way sharing tips, advice, honest feedback of the highs and lows of running your own business, and giving you access to the exciting world of ecommerce.

One of the biggest realisations I've had about growing my own ecommerce business, is that it is a constantly evolving journey. I encourage you to use this book as a living, breathing resource that you can turn to at any point in your journey.

You will find this book has more impact on your life when you use it regularly as a guide as you navigate the road ahead. Have a notebook and pen handy, and I encourage you to highlight all the words that resonate with you. Most importantly, take action on the exercises I've created for you—after all, without action, your goals are simply wishes.

I've poured my heart and soul into crafting this book to ensure you get value and practical action steps you can apply in your life or business right away. I draw from my own experiences and share with you the invaluable lessons I've learnt along the way, as well as some I am still learning today.

Before we get into it, I want to let you know there are moments in this book where I'm also very open about my recent struggles with anxiety and burnout. It can be easy to feel like you need to have everything together all of the time; however, the truth is that building a business and raising a family is tough, and it's okay to struggle sometimes. In this book, I open up about my own battles with anxiety and burnout, and share the strategies that have helped me to manage these challenges and maintain my mental health while growing my business and being a single parent.

I encourage you to use this book as a working document that you can use to make notes to follow up on concepts, work through the activities and further develop your own ideas. One of my mentors taught me this simple formula to use when you are reading something, attending a workshop or in a meeting. Use an 'A' for any notes that require you to take action, use 'I' for any ideas you think of, and 'R' to research something later. Try using the AIR notetaking method throughout this book.

Being self-made

Running a business can be challenging and isolating—it's also one of the most rewarding experiences you can have. I'm honoured to be able to share my insights and stories with you in the hopes that they help you achieve the success and fulfilment you deserve, while feeling less alone along the way.

I called this book *Self-Made* because the term has always held meaning for me. To some, 'self-made' may suggest a measure of financial success or achievement, but to me, it's so much more than that.

For me, being self-made is about having the resilience, self-belief and determination to create the life you desire, regardless of your obstacles or current circumstances. It's about not losing hope in yourself or your vision, even when others (or you yourself!) have doubts. It's when the path ahead seems uncertain, but you decide to be brave, vulnerable and courageous anyway.

It's when you start to experience a level of financial success and financial independence, but don't lose sight of your deepest values, and you stay aligned to your truest self and your purpose. It's not feeling as though you need to be more, have more or do more in order to be successful or appear successful to strangers on the internet. Ultimately, being self-made is having the freedom to choose to live life on your terms, to be able to make a meaningful impact and to feel a sense of immense gratitude for the life you have built for yourself.

Throughout my life, I have faced a number of personal and professional setbacks and challenges that could have easily derailed my dreams. But through hard work, a strong mindset, perseverance, lots of self-healing work and a stubborn refusal to give up, I have been able to create a successful business that has brought joy and beauty to countless people worldwide, and continues to pay it forward and spread kindness.

I believe that being self-made is a mindset that anyone can learn and adopt, regardless of your background or circumstance. It's about getting honest with where you are right now, taking ownership and accountability of your life and your future, and working tirelessly and doing whatever it takes to make your dreams a reality.

This book is your very own guide to success. A guide that will empower you to achieve your goals and live your own version of a fulfilling, self-made life.

So, whether you're just starting out with your own business, desire to start your own business, have been running your own business for years or are currently facing hardship of some sort, I invite you now to dive into the pages of this book and get started on creating the success you desire.

Olivia

1

Seizing sliding door moments

How making hard decisions can transform your path

Whether you are reading this book because you want to start your own business or you already have a business, I am going to share as much of my experiences of building small businesses with you in this book—both the good and the bad. Nothing in life worth having comes easy; however, when it comes to business and social media, there is so much comparison and misinformation around how challenging it is to run a small business. If you are struggling with self-doubt, a lack of belief in your ability to build a big life from your small business, concerns about managing your cash flow or any of the thousands of other worries you have as a small business owner, I want to start by acknowledging you are not alone in feeling like this.

If you are getting ready to start a business, I also want to prepare you as much as possible for what may be ahead, and how you can better prepare yourself for what it takes to run a small business (see figure 1.1 for what constitutes a small business). This book will focus primarily on ecommerce founders. Ecommerce is a broad category that covers a range of industries, such as beauty, wellness, fashion, accessories, electronics and other industries that trade online.

WHAT IS A SMALL BUSINESS?

Micro business	<10 employees
Small business	10-19 employees
Small-medium-sized business	<249 employees
Large business	>250 employees

Figure 1.1 what is a small business?

Taking your first steps

In this chapter, I cover the very first step to starting a business: *making the decision*. Choosing to start your own business is one of the most exciting, yet terrifying, decisions you will ever make in your life, especially if this is going to be your full-time career and not a side business. It means you have to fully back yourself and be prepared to be solely responsible for securing your own income.

That is not an easy decision to make, and so often it's the very reason why many people don't take the leap to start their own business or move from having a side business to it being their full-time career. The sheer thought of having to solely rely on yourself and your own efforts to generate enough income to survive is daunting. Some of you will have a bigger appetite for risk than others, and everyone's personal situations are different, which also plays a big factor in whether or not you choose to start a business. I have always had a very large appetite for risk, and a strong ability to back myself (even without a plan), but I recognise through my journey of mentoring women, that this is not a common attitude. It is possible to start your own business without this level of confidence.

It's also important to know that there is no shame or guilt should you choose to close or sell your business. Just like with relationships, people come into our lives for a reason, season or a lifetime, and the same should be said about business. Sometimes the first business you run may not succeed (this is more common than not), but it will teach you so much about yourself and about business. Every failure in life is a lesson, and we learn more from our failures than we do our successes.

I wish I had access to a book like this when I made the tough decision to close my first business in 2009, and I wish I had read a book like this before leaving my full-time role as a general manager in 2015 to launch Shhh Silk. Hindsight is a beautiful thing; however, so is life experience and the lessons you learn along the way.

There are some important sliding door moments in my life that I want to share with you because I haven't always been self-made. In fact, up until my early 30s, I was still stuck in my old money psychology mindset that money is scarce and hard to earn, and I'm not good with money. I didn't grow up around money and neither of my parents were entrepreneurs. My parents were both working-class people with multiple low-income jobs. I grew up watching them work extremely hard, and yet never seem to have any money. So what changed? I started making different choices; I decided to choose a different story for my life.

Life and business are about choices: some you make consciously and others, unconsciously. And some choices or decisions are much harder to make than others. Some choices will change the course of your journey, and in my case, can absolutely allow you to go from drowning in debt to becoming self-made. For me, whenever it comes to making a decision or choosing between multiple outcomes, whether in business or in my personal life, it really comes down to being prepared to deal with the consequences of the decision.

Let me share a story with you about the toughest decision I have faced in my life so far. That decision went on to reshape my life, my mindset and my mental toughness for every future decision I've made, and taught me how to go from having nothing to becoming self-made.

LIFE LESSON 1
Don't always choose the easy door

My sliding door moment came in the early summer of 2000. I was 19 and had recently been crowned Miss Tropicana Gold Coast 2000. I was studying acting at The Australian Film and Television Academy on the Gold Coast.

After being crowned Miss Tropicana Gold Coast, one of your duties is to attend different nightclubs and promotional events. One Thursday night, I was at an iconic Surfers Paradise pub where they used to serve $1 spirits. I was at the bar when a stranger asked me if I was taken. Before I could answer, I felt someone put their arms around me from behind and respond, 'Yes, she is. She's with me.'

Those six innocent words used as a pick-up line would change my life forever. When I turned around, I discovered the man who had said them was a friend of my cousin who lived on the Gold Coast.

He had long dark hair and was a few years older than me. He looked like trouble and the rebellious 19-year-old teenager in me was instantly hooked. After far too many $1 spirits, I went home with the man from the bar with the long dark hair and we spent a drunken night together.

Not long after, I graduated from The Australian Film and Television Academy and was busy preparing my application for the National Institute of Dramatic Arts (NIDA) summer-school program, the most prestigious acting school in the country.

I have studied acting professionally since I was nine years old. At that time, acting was my life. It was all I thought about and all I dreamt about. It's why I chose to leave school at 16 to pursue studying acting.

My lifestyle on the Gold Coast during this time was young, wild and carefree!

I would surf during the day, go out with friends most nights and consume a lot of alcohol in the evenings. It was like schoolies, but seven nights a week, all year long—I had no responsibilities and not a care in the world.

In December 2000, I was on such a high as I had just been accepted into the summer-school program for NIDA. I was in, and now I was one step closer to living out my dream and moving to Hollywood.

The moment when everything changed

Enter my first sliding door moment. It was my sister's idea that I take a pregnancy test as I had missed my period. I was less concerned as I put it down to the heavy partying I had been doing and a lack of sleep. When I saw the result, I collapsed on the floor of the bathroom and cried for what felt like an eternity. There was no way I was pregnant! I had only just turned 19 and I was on the pill. The pregnancy test had to be wrong. I was in denial; I was also in shock. I booked an appointment with a GP who confirmed I was pregnant and sent me off for an ultrasound to work out the gestation of my unborn child. I couldn't process anything; it all felt like I was watching someone else's life and not my own.

So many thoughts and emotions were running through my body. In the midst of experiencing all of this shock and emotion, I knew deep within my soul that I was going to have this baby.

To this day, that deep knowing is hard for me to explain, but as soon as I accepted I was pregnant, as devastated and absolutely gutted as I was about not going to NIDA summer school, I knew I had to keep this baby. This was my sliding door moment. This decision was going to reshape my future.

Telling my parents was the hardest part. My dad was born and raised in Scotland in the 1940s and he was very strict. I had never even been allowed to have a boy over at my house, and now I had to tell him I was pregnant!

The thought of sharing this news with my parents terrified me. I waited a few weeks, and then I called home. My mum answered the phone and I said, 'I have something to tell you. I'm pregnant', and then I think I just hung up. I didn't take my parents' calls for a few days after that. When I finally did answer their call, it was my dad, and the first words he said were, 'Come home; we will support you.'

I will never forget how supported I felt in that moment. With all of the fear I was feeling, having already decided I was keeping this baby, it was so nice to feel as though I wasn't going to be alone.

Making hard choices

I didn't move home, not straight away. I really wanted to try and make things work with my baby's father. I moved into his parents' garage with him in the middle of the Queensland summer. I had the worst morning sickness—I have never understood why they call it morning sickness, as I was sick day and night. And the garage was so hot. I remember thinking that I couldn't raise my baby in a garage. I was so grateful to his parents for accepting me into their home under the circumstances, but I felt we needed to get a place of our own and try and make this work.

I was 19 and he was 23—we were both so young. I had no savings and no idea how expensive it was going to be to bring a child into the world. But I was certain at the time that I would make it work; I just had to.

We moved into an apartment in Miami on the Gold Coast. The good thing about living on the Gold Coast in 2001 was that renting an apartment was relatively inexpensive. It felt good to have our own place; now we just needed to see if this relationship could work.

I don't remember the small things from that time in my life, like what we ate for dinner or who cooked. I remember he would go out with his mates and I would stay home. I know I wasn't happy, and I knew the relationship wasn't working. The plan to leave and move back to my parents' home in Victoria felt like the right decision, but how? I started to feel very alone and trapped. I knew I needed to leave, but I was scared.

I spoke to my parents and we agreed I needed to come home, so when I was seven months' pregnant, I told him I was going home to visit my parents, and I never returned.

The following few months were traumatising to say the least. Naturally, he didn't take the news well over the phone that I was not returning to Queensland and I no longer wanted to be in a relationship with him. It wasn't until years later that I fully understood the impact the traumatic events that took place during the early years of my daughter's life, between her father and I, had on me, and the significant impact they had on my future relationships.

When I first found out I was pregnant, I was so focused on my decision to have this child, I never stopped to process what it would be like if I was going to do it alone.

Motherhood moments

I gave birth to my healthy daughter, Georgia Rose, ten days past her due date.

Life as a new mum was exhausting. Between trying to learn how to breastfeed properly and the constant interrupted sleep, the days soon felt like groundhog day. My mum and my sister were both amazing supports for me in the early stages of Georgia's life, and gave me the opportunity to get back to the gym and just have a moment to myself.

Aside from the mental, emotional and physical exhaustion of being a new mum, I soon realised the financial strain having a child at such a young age would have on my life. (More about that later.)

It was only recently during a podcast interview when we were talking about my life as a young mum that I recalled a moment I was at my lowest. Georgia was a few months old, and she was in the back of the car crying nonstop, and I didn't think I could go on. I had a vision of my life ending, and until recently, I never understood what that moment was. I was most likely experiencing postnatal depression (PND)—not something that was well known or spoken about in 2001. According to the Black Dog Institute, postnatal depression:

> describes the more severe or prolonged symptoms of depression (clinical depression) that last more than two weeks and interfere with the ability to function with normal routines on a daily basis including caring for a baby.[1]

The same article goes on to say that around 14 per cent of women in Australia experience PND and that of those women, the symptoms of PND begin in pregnancy in around 40 per cent of cases.

How did I cope without knowing what I was likely experiencing? Honestly, not very well. I would go out on weekends with friends and drink my realities away for the night.

Motherhood was a challenging first couple of years for me: balancing being a young single mother; working full time in real estate; and trying to stay connected to my youth, my friends and enjoy the life of a young person.

Sliding doors

My motherhood journey has been incredibly tough in some parts, which I am going to share in the following chapters; however, it has also forced me to be resilient, resourceful and determined from a very young age.

Over the past 22 years, I have had a couple of moments where I have wondered what my life would be like now if I chose differently that day back in December 2000. Would I have made it as an actress? Would I be a famous TV or movie star? Would I have suffered the same financial situation? These are answers I will never know. And, truthfully, my teenage dreams no longer feel aligned to my life's purpose. What I do know is, my daughter chose me. This was the path I believe I was supposed to take in life. After all, life doesn't happen to us, it happens for us!

So, when it comes to sliding door moments or making tough choices in your life or with your career or business, I don't believe that the easy door is always the right door. For me, it's often the unknown door or the toughest door that you choose to walk through that presents the most opportunity for growth. Choosing to always take the path of least resistance, or the easiest door, can be useful in some scenarios; however, when it comes to building character and learning to grow through facing challenges and overcoming obstacles, the path of least resistance is rarely the choice I go with. Nothing in life worth having should be easy; everything good in life requires some effort.

Yes, choosing to make the tough choice rather than the easy choice can mean you may face temporary hardship or challenges that you may not have imagined, but they don't have to be permanent. It's the growth that exists on the *other* side of the door that you need to consider. Choosing to become your own boss, choosing to be self-made, is absolutely going to come with some challenges and setbacks in your life, but unless you choose to take a risk and back yourself, you're also never going to know how *big* your life can really become.

I have learnt some techniques or strategies over the years that have helped me to make tough decisions. Grab your notebook and pen and let's begin our first activity together.

ACTIVITY

How to make a tough decision

Think of a situation that involves you needing to make a decision that you have been putting off. Maybe it's changing careers, leaving your job, starting a business or hiring your first team member. Write the scenario down in as much detail as you can.

Ask yourself *why* making a decision about this is important to you.

Now make a list of all of the possible outcomes that may arise based on your decision to do this or not to do this. Cover off both the good and challenging.

Ask yourself: Does the scenario you are attempting to make a decision about align with your goals or vision for your life?

Looking at all of the possible outcomes you have written down about your decision, are there things you can think of that would help to alleviate any potential risk?

Are you *ready* to make a decision?

If not, what is *stopping* you from making a decision. And remember, making no decision is still a decision. It may indicate you're not ready.

If you are ready, review your answers to these questions and you should feel a sense of clarity or reassurance about which decision feels most aligned to you right now.

Feeling the discomfort of a big decision

It's important to remember that the right decision is not always the easiest or the one with the least risk. It is usually the one that you feel offers you the most growth, and will push you towards a more successful and fulfilled life. Staying in your comfort zone and being afraid to make changes in your life will lead to you staying in the same place that you are right now. In order to move towards living a self-made life, you need to get comfortable with being uncomfortable and really backing yourself. It doesn't mean you have to go all in without first stopping and reviewing your decision or at least thinking about what the potential consequences or outcomes may be, it just means not letting fear of the unknown stop you. You need to accept some level of discomfort, as it's through those moments that we grow and evolve.

Looking back at my earlier years, what helped me get through some of the tougher days was simply choosing to keep going, despite how hard life felt at that moment. I had a strong belief that my situation was not permanent, and that it would all lead me to a better place.

No matter where you currently are in your journey, no matter how hard things feel at any moment, choosing to keep going is far easier when you have a strong belief that your current situation isn't permanent. There's a quote I love by Nido Qubein that says: 'Your present circumstances don't determine where you can go; they merely determine where you start.'

So it's about finding a way through what you are experiencing. That can be seeking support or help, it can be choosing to let go of certain people or influences in your life or it can be just telling yourself 'you've got this', and then doing one thing each day to bring you closer to where you want to be. You do need to commit to moving forward, and this book will help you to make some positive changes in your life.

If you are doing it tough with your own business right now, you can use this book as a guide to help you out of your current situation and to rebuild your business from the ground up.

There are no rules with business. You are allowed to change your business model, pivot at any moment, do whatever it takes to make your business and yourself a success. Don't let old thinking or fear of what others will think hold you back.

I am currently in the process, eight years into building Shhh Silk, of re-evaluating our entire business model, and asking myself the very questions I am challenging you to ask yourself. I am not a master at business, but I am a master at doing whatever it takes to build a bigger and better life for myself. A life on my own terms—a self-made life. You have permission at any stage to do this too.

Sometimes that will mean changing course, making challenging but necessary decisions, and steering your life and your business in a new direction.

Despite me not knowing all of the potential consequences and hardships that would come as a result of choosing to be a young, single mother, the decision to choose that door turned out to be my life's biggest growth opportunity. And it continues to be the reason for some of my biggest lessons and successes in my life so far. It has taught me how to be resilient, determined, tenacious, driven, resourceful, strong, independent, optimistic and mentally tough, and encouraged me to start and grow several businesses, write this book, purchase my own properties, have the life experience to mentor other women and go on to create financial independence for myself by the age of 40. It was not an overnight process, but with a commitment to daily action, I achieved all of this in under two decades.

If not now, when?

Deciding when it is time to make the choice to launch your business or make a big life change is a tough one. Because truthfully, there really isn't such a thing as a right time. There will always be many variables to consider, and knowing that the timing will always feel slightly off should reassure you.

Take writing this book as an example. For me, the timing couldn't have been worse. I committed to writing this book in November 2022, just a month or so prior to the economic slowdown in retail in Australia. A time where, as a business owner, I needed to dedicate more time and focus to my business as sales were rapidly declining. And finding the extra two hours a day (or more at times) it would take for the next 11 months to write, edit and launch this book was going to be a massive challenge.

I chose to do it at that time as I believe the lessons and tips in this book are both timely and more relevant now than ever. I also wanted to share the journey of business with you while facing challenges myself. I know women need a resource like this to help them grow their brands now more than ever.

You *can* always find a way to achieve success, as long as your goals align with your values—and you need to really want it. It's not enough to wish for success without putting in the effort, time and focus to achieve it. This is the magic of choosing the hard door—in my experience, there's usually something incredible waiting for you on the other side. It may just take some time, and some work, for you to see the results of choosing the hard door.

It's important to remember life is messy, fun, hard, exhilarating, precious, but above all, life is short. Choose your door, and enjoy the ride.

2

Rewriting your money story

The key to overcoming financial challenges

You might have a big dream for your business but you're not sure how to get there. Ultimately a successful business starts with getting your personal finances in order.

I can still remember what it felt like being in over $100 000 of debt in my 20s (the equivalent of about $140 000 today). Going from one personal loan to multiple maxed-out credit cards, mounting unpaid amenity bills, overdue day care fees, over 200 enforcement warrants and hundreds of unpaid CityLink fines.

Feeling as though I was no longer in control of my finances felt both terrifying and suffocating. When I was experiencing severe financial difficulty, that feeling never really left me. It was there the moment I woke up in the morning, and it was still there when I went to bed at night. It felt as though there was no escaping it. Well, at least this is how I remember it feeling for me for the best part of 14 years. And while in this chapter I am going to talk a lot about what I have done to turn my financial situation around and work on my mental relationship with money, there are still moments where I find myself falling back into old patterns of thinking about money.

I still use the same tips I am sharing with you to reset my own relationship and thinking with money to allow me to create more wealth and financial freedom in my life. When it comes to the financial situation of my business, I use these tools to allow me to continue growing Shhh Silk (even when the economy is tough).

A word of caution

While a lot of the tips in this chapter will help you gain a sense of control over your finances, it is important to remember that I am not a financial adviser. I am sharing strategies that worked for me based on my individual circumstances and experiences, strategies that ultimately allowed me to escape crippling financial hardship. You should always seek independent financial advice for your individual needs.

Let's explore how I was able to climb my way out of such high debt. Firstly, it took me over ten years to learn and practice these strategies, as I was not exposed to any financial literacy, knowledge or insights when I was growing up. I only learnt how to better understand and manage finances as I crossed paths with different mentors in my life, and started teaching myself about money.

If you are currently finding your financial situation challenging, some of what I experienced may resonate with you, and more importantly, it may provide you with the hope and comfort that it is possible to turn your current financial situation around.

LIFE LESSON 2

My rock bottom: facing jail time for my mounting debts

The year 2020 was a big year of self-reflection for me. I reflected on my childhood, my earliest memories, my friendships, my relationships, my health, my finances, my boundaries, my career, my family and how I wanted to spend my days going forward.

Some of my earliest childhood memories are a love for exploring nature, making mud pies and tadpole fishing with my sister, and my love for horses. The darker memories are of feeling unsafe in a volatile household with a father who drank too much when he was younger and regularly verbally abused my mother. My parents struggled financially, even though they were both working multiple jobs to try and pay their mortgage. They purchased their first home in the 1980s when interest rates were as high as 20%, the equivalent of buying a home on a credit card in today's world. As a child, I never went without shelter, food or clothing, but I do remember not understanding why I couldn't have the same toys, school lunch orders or material things that my friends had.

Money stories

While money was tight at home, and my parents were living from pay cheque to pay cheque, they would still manage to take my sister and me on a road trip every second year, and there were always gifts under the Christmas tree. Experiencing these imprints during my formative years led to the money story I developed as my truth, which was, *money is tight, money is not in abundance, there are always more bills to pay than there is money.*

These and hundreds more examples just like it shaped my money stories, and my psychology and beliefs around money. In a *Forbes* article, writer Michael Kay describes your money story as something foundational to how you think about money, how you react to money and how you communicate about money.[2] For those who grew up where conflict was a central theme, any conversation dealing with money begins with a stomach-ache. For those who grew up in the dark around money, dealing with the mysteries of money in adulthood is likely to be a struggle.

My earliest money story was that I would always have to create my own money if I wanted extra things. This story started quite young, around age six or seven, when I would walk door to door and sell homemade perfume to neighbours for $3 a bottle. Or I would set up garage stalls at the end of the driveway and sell toys I no longer played with in exchange for small change that I would use at the milk bar or at the local fish-and-chip shop near the school where I would purchase a $2 mix (chips, dim sim and potato cake).

I never saved any of the money I made as a child or when I worked four jobs as a teenager. Due to my scarcity mindset,

I would spend every dollar I made. Reflecting back on my own money habits at a young age, saving money was not something that I practiced, nor something I had experienced in my own family environment. This behaviour continued well into my adult years, and it wasn't until 2020, while going through a lot of self-reflection work, that I decided to rewrite my own personal money story: my relationship and mindset with money.

When COVID hit the shores in Australia in March 2020, it also forced me to completely restructure the way in which I ran the cash flow management (or lack of cash flow management) with my business.

Let's go a little bit deeper here. By the age of 21, as a single mother with a two-year-old daughter, I was beginning to drown in debt. I was working full time in real estate, however, due to my low income, my earnings did not cover my expenses, let alone my discretionary spending habits. I was paying out-of-pocket child care fees, rent, a car loan, credit card repayments, food, utility bills, petrol, clothing for my daughter, road tolls and so on.

It was while I was working in real estate that I met my first influential mentor, Andrew. Andrew was a real estate agent roughly ten years older than me, and it became apparent to me years later that he had a completely different money story to me. I remember he owned a BMW 7 Series, and it even had a phone inside! (This was back in 2004.) I had never seen a car like this in my life; not only was it impressive it was immaculately clean inside.

I remember my first ride in this car, and I remember that Tracy Chapman was playing. To this day, whenever I feel as though I need to reset my money mindset or energy,

I play Tracy Chapman on Spotify with a smile on my face. Not only did Andrew introduce me to the power of self-development, reading and sales, he also showed me that there is no magic wand or secret formula that makes anyone less or more deserving of financial freedom. *It is a 100% mindset.* It does, however, as I discovered, take ownership and action on your part to change how you are operating and thinking in regard to finances. Andrew had a portfolio of real estate at a young age, but more importantly, it was his mindset and approach to wealth and life that intrigued me.

Here are some things that I still practice today that I learnt from my time being mentored by Andrew. These cost little to nothing, but can help with your money story and money mindset.

1. A clear environment = a clear head

Having a messy exterior environment is often a reflection of what's going on internally. Our outside is a reflection of our inside. It costs nothing to keep your car, your home and your office tidy. It is often starting with these small daily disciplines and actions that lead to much bigger results in your life.

Disclaimer: This lesson wasn't instantaneous for me, and truth be told, I didn't start to respect my environment until I was in my late 20s or early 30s. Introduce this daily habit into your life and you will notice things start to shift for you and your mindset.

2. Always have petrol in your car

Okay I know this advice sounds really obvious, however, Andrew rescued me when I had an empty tank too many times to remember. I am happy to say this is a habit I have now taught my adult daughter. Never let your car run empty. When I reflected back to why I used to run out of petrol so much when I was in my 20s, it had more to do with my finances not being in order, which just added to the chaotic energy I was operating in, and served as part of my victim mentality storytelling.

Truthfully, this tip is less about your car and more a reminder that allowing yourself to run out of petrol regularly, run late with bills or even be late to appointments is not helpful in reshaping your mindset about money and managing finances, both of which you will need to learn in order to successfully run a business. The more discipline you can introduce into your day-to-day life (i.e. taking care of the small things), the easier it is to manage the big things.

3. Invest in your self-development

If you only have $5 to spend, rather than buying a latte or a croissant, invest that money into a secondhand self-development book or audiobook. You can watch the $5 grow and multiply as your new mindset starts to take hold. Reading self-development books was one of the earliest strategies I adopted when I was drowning in debt. The benefits are that you gain new perspectives on things you have no prior experience in. Learning that other people have experienced adversity and setbacks, and have worked their way out of it, can be a powerful way for you to create change in your life. I still read several books a month, have a coach, see a therapist, take courses and seek out mentors.

I owe a lot of my success and mindset shifts to Andrew. I am immensely grateful for him taking me under his wing and showing me a different way. But that different way starts and continues inside your own head. My success today would not be possible if it weren't for the hundreds of books, audiobooks, podcasts, interviews, TED Talks and so on that I have read or listened to and then applied in my own life.

Here are some of my favourite self-development books:

The Universe Has Your Back by Gabrielle Bernstein
You Are a Badass at Making Money by Jen Sincero
The 4-Hour Work Week by Tim Ferriss
The Miracle Morning by Hal Elrod
8 Rules of Love by Jay Shetty
The Barefoot Investor by Scott Pape
A Course in Miracles by Dr Helen Schucman
Super Attractor by Gabrielle Bernstein

There are so many different ways to digest mindset content today, whether it be YouTube, audiobooks, TED Talks, social media or books. Technology means there has never been an easier or more cost-effective way to explore self-development. Commit to spending at least four hours a week on consuming content that has a positive effect on your growth and mindset, and this will have a direct result on your current and future life.

Dealing with debt

The road out of debt was a slow, often dark road for me. By the age of 26, I was over $100 000 in debt, partly from the several credit cards I had obtained in my early 20s, and partly from my hundreds of unpaid bills.

What started out as one $2000 credit card, soon became several credit cards, often used to pay out other existing credit cards (not a good trap to fall into). The day came when I defaulted on an old credit card and simply could not pay it off. The debt collection letters kept coming, the calls soon followed and then the dreaded day that destroyed my credit rating for the next seven years: the first default on my personal credit file.

At the time I remember thinking it wasn't that big of a deal, and I was somewhat relieved that it was one less bill to worry about. Little did I know at the time, those marks on my credit file would follow me well into my early 30s. It was around this time that I started a constant merry-go-round mindset of bill after bill, and payment plan after payment plan. I had lost any sense of the seriousness of my financial situation. If you can relate to any of this, I encourage you to do whatever it takes to change your mindset about your current financial situation and *do not ignore it*. It will only get worse, and you can start to make this situation better. But doing the same things over and over and expecting a different outcome won't work. You need a circuit breaker. You need to do something differently and that is take ownership, responsibility and accountability. It's time to take *small daily actions* towards climbing your way out of this situation.

The victim mindset I played out in my head for years, of me being the poor young, pregnant, single 19-year-old mum, was really just a mask so I wouldn't have to take ownership of my finances. It was me refusing to see there could be another way. The turning point for me was the day I had to go to the Melbourne Magistrates' Court over my unpaid CityLink toll debt, which by my early 30s was over $70 000! *WTF*, I can hear you say. *How on earth does someone have that amount of unpaid CityLink tolls?* Oh, believe me, writing this, I am getting a weird sensation in my neck as I relive those memories.

I was honestly so scared that day, as I wasn't sure if prison was a real possibility for me. Luckily, I was allowed to leave the courtroom with an incredibly high monthly payment plan in place that, again, would send my monthly budget into turmoil. Where would I find the extra $3000 a month to pay the debt back? This was it, though. There was no more mucking around and no more ignoring the situation that had been escalating for the previous decade. I would now have to work out how to manage a budget, change my spending habits and do things differently. I was not going back into that courtroom!

So how did I get there?

I need to explain to you how I ended up with this level of debt. CityLink tolls start off as a few dollars per trip, or monthly bills of maybe $100, and as I was earning less at the time than my fixed expenses, things such as my toll bills would go untouched for months and even years! It's possible that a single $7 toll trip can end up costing you $300+ after the Magistrates' Courts and the warrant fees. I often joke that I have paid for part of the CityLink road and should have a plaque in my name. But it's nothing to laugh about. What is important to address is that I could have avoided these tolls by, firstly, not using the toll roads and choosing a longer, but free route. This is the level of accountability you need to take with your personal and your business finances.

If you can't afford the very things adding to your financial strain, you need to remove them from your life and your business. Going to Pilates is nice, but if you are stretched to pay your bills, then you need to choose a more affordable exercise option, or a free one until you have the cash to afford it. For me, this has been one of the most fascinating lessons about my relationship to money. For years I resisted setting a budget as it felt restrictive and controlling. It felt like I would be missing out. But what I failed to see was just how empowering a budget would be for my life. How, instead of controlling me, it enables me to create and build wealth for myself. This is one of the biggest mindset shifts some people need to experience for themselves when it comes to managing money. That, just like in business, as the saying goes *if you fail to plan, you plan to fail.* A budget or a money management system is your money empowerment and wealth creation plan. It's your map of how you can go from $0 to whatever that dollar number looks like for you. Getting myself out of extreme debt (which I am so thrilled to say I finally did in 2015) was exactly the same process I use today when saving or investing.

Note: It took me over 14 years of constant mindset work, along with the commitment to work my way out of debt, but once I got there, I was able to start rewriting the next chapters of my life, including starting Shhh Silk. It also took another five years of mindset work to start reshaping my relationship with money, and really start to introduce this into my business. As you'll read in the following chapters, just because I climbed my way out of debt, didn't mean I knew how to manage money, and this would be another costly mistake.

Five steps to financial independence

So to recap, here are the fundamental steps I took to get on top of my debt (illustrated in figure 2.1):

Figure 2.1 five steps to financial independence

1. Take ownership

In the words of Brené Brown, 'When we deny our stories, they define us. When we own our stories, we get to write a brave new ending.' Choosing to replay the victim card over and over again in your head will only keep you a victim. It's hard, but it's necessary to take a good hard look in the mirror, own your situation and commit yourself to rewriting a new chapter for your life. You also need to refrain from judging yourself for the situation you or your business may be in. Just take ownership.

You may be wondering how this step will bring in the extra finances or shifts needed to pay down your debts, but that's not for you to worry about at this early stage. Just keep focusing on what is coming, reminding yourself that what you need is on its way.

2. Read and listen to mindset content

Training your mind is no different to training your body. Just as your body needs 30 minutes of exercise a day to maintain health, so does your mind. But even if you start with ten minutes a day, that will start to make your situation more manageable, and you will start making the necessary steps to get on top of your debts.

I recommend doing this first thing in the morning. This is where *The Miracle Morning* book and practice can create incredible shifts in your life. Choose to listen to or consume content that is empowering for you. Meditations about wealth and attracting abundance can be powerful tools to help you shift your current mindset. It costs nothing to do mindset training: you don't need an expensive gym membership or a personal trainer, you just need a good YouTube meditation on positive mindset or manifesting abundance, and you will be on your way to rewriting your story.

3. Open your bills

This sounds silly, but for some people, depending on the level of debt you are currently in, you no longer even open your bills. You need to commit to moving out of denial and avoidance and into accountability and ownership. This step took me years to do, hence my CityLink fines moving from a few dollars to hundreds of dollars each. I was ignoring the bills rather than dealing with them one by one. I could have saved myself tens of thousands of dollars if I had opened them and then followed the next step.

4. Set up payment plans

Whether it's your personal debts or your business debts (or both), the first tactical thing you need to do is call every single creditor or business that you owe money to and request a payment plan. You need to make sure you start as small as you can. As someone who has used payment plans for over a decade, the more you default, the harder these plans are to reinstate. This can then put you in a position where you need to pay the full amount immediately. If this step is too hard for you emotionally or mentally, reach out to a trusted friend or family member and ask them to take care of this step for you. My mentor and friend Andrew first took this step off my hands, and set up my first ever payment plans for me in my 20s.

5. *Ask for help*

This was the hardest step of all for me. I had a lot of shame and guilt around my debt, and I used to hide as much as I could from my friends and family. But here's the thing: your debt does not define you. It does not define the wonderful person you are, and it does not define your worth. I know it can feel like it does, but it doesn't.

You may have never been shown how to manage money (like me), so I strongly encourage you to reach out to someone you trust, whether it's a friend, peer or family member, and share your situation with them. This is also helpful as it allows people to support your goals in getting out of debt, and means you can explain why gift giving, going to dinner and so on all need to be pulled back for a while as you work towards building your wealth.

The other thing that happens when you ask for help is that people often have ways in which they can and want to help you. And you need to accept their help. This is why I am such an advocate for helping others, for all of the love, support, kindness and financial help I have received in my life. You will pay it forward one day as you'll have felt how incredible it feels to receive support from others.

Saving for a rainy day

Now, the last thing I want to share is the importance of having an emergency fund once you are on top of your finances. An emergency fund is something you can read more about online or in books like *The Barefoot Investor.* Essentially, it's your emergency money for life's unforeseen or unplanned moments. Start small, but start. Even $10 a week is a start, and you'll be amazed how committing to financial savings becomes easier the more you do it. Let money flow, start to reflect on and remove your old money stories from your past experiences and create new money stories.

If you want to learn more about money stories, read Melissa Browne's book *Budgets Don't Work (But This Does).* This book empowered me to once again be vulnerable, and not only own my money story, but share it with you in the hope that you see that it is possible to rewrite your own ending when it comes to finances.

Stop thinking debt, start thinking prosperity.

3

Roadmap to success

Six key traits of a self-made entrepreneur

I was born an entrepreneur; I have always had a natural tendency to want to take risks from a young age and have found it easy to connect and talk to people. I started my first physical shop at the end of my driveway when I was only five years old, and even at that young age, I had the instinct to make a handwritten sign and put it at the end of our long road to alert passers-by to come and visit my shop (garage sale).

I would get up early and set up my table with my preloved toys, stuffed animals and books with pride, merchandising it so that it was easy for customers to see what was for sale and how much things cost. I remember the feeling I would get each time I successfully negotiated a sale with a customer. It was more about that feeling to me than the money I would make at the end of the long day.

Being an entrepreneur, or wanting to become an entrepreneur, is an internal feeling. Deep down in your soul you crave the freedom to turn your dreams and visions into reality. To create something that no one else can see except you (initially). It's the ultimate creation: you get to create whatever it is that you can see in your mind. Well, at least this is how it has always felt for me.

In this chapter we are going to explore some traits that I have developed to become a self-made business owner. These traits are learned behaviours and will make the path to success much easier and more enjoyable for you.

The six essential traits of self-made entrepreneurs

Becoming a self-made entrepreneur takes a lot of work, but there are also specific traits you will need if you're going to transition from startup to success (illustrated in figure 3.1).

1. Clear vision and purpose

What is it you're trying to create? How can you share and express this vision to others? What does success look like? What is the purpose of your brand? It's important to have a clear vision and purpose for your business so you can communicate your vision effectively, and you can inspire and motivate stakeholders, including your employees, investors and customers. By understanding and communicating your brand's purpose, your target audience can resonate with your brand. It also helps to build loyalty and differentiate your business in a competitive market.

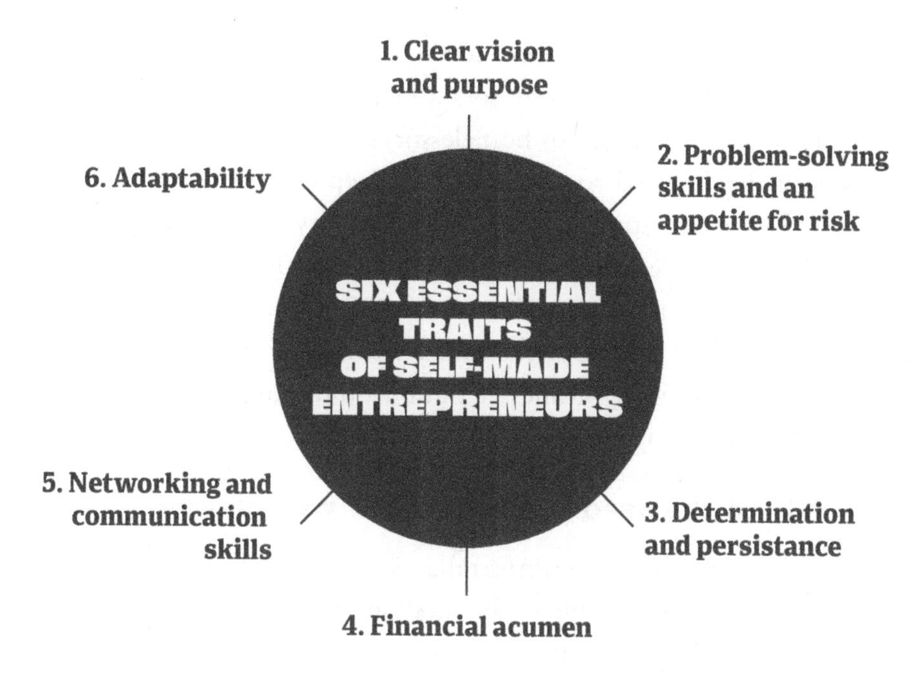

Figure 3.1 six essential traits of self-made entrepreneurs

LIFE LESSON 3
Follow your dreams

I had the vision of my silk pillowcase brand Shhh Silk in July 2015 after returning home from a trip to New York with my family. I had left my role as a general manager just one month earlier, and had decided to use my time in the States to work out what my next business would be.

A big part of my vision for Shhh Silk has always been to pay it forward and do good. I knew this would be the case no matter what brand I created. On our first night in New York, as we were leaving our hotel to go for a walk, my eight-year-old son and I had a conversation about the prevalence of homelessness. It was the first time he had witnessed so many people sleeping rough on the cold concrete streets of this beautiful city. He asked me why they were sleeping on the ground. In that moment, I couldn't find an answer that seemed big enough to answer his innocent question. Instead, I made a promise to my son that the next business I built would make a positive difference to people's lives.

Where the seed for Shhh Silk was planted

After a long flight from Australia, we were tired and the jet lag was setting in. One of the small luxuries I look forward to most when getting ready for a good night's sleep is resting my head on my silk pillowcase. My silk pillowcase comes with me everywhere; just like my toiletries, it is a non-negotiable. I put my white silk pillowcase over my hotel pillow and attempted to sleep off some of the jet lag. The next day we went for a long walk around Central Park, and when we returned to the hotel later that day, I noticed my silk pillowcase had been removed by housekeeping.

I went down to reception to ask how to get my silk pillowcase back. I was genuinely heartbroken when the front desk explained that they outsource the laundry, and I wouldn't be able to retrieve my silk pillowcase. I knew it had been done in error, but I was devastated as I had slept on a silk pillowcase every night for years. What had started out as a recommendation from my hairdresser to protect my hair and blow-dries had become so much more than that to me. It had become a nightly comfort, a physical calming sensation I looked forward to experiencing at the end of a long day.

I accepted it was gone and was slightly irritated that I would now need to invest another $100 to replace it while I was travelling. This never happened though as in 2015 there were no silk pillowcases sold in any major department stores in the USA. Sleeping on a cotton pillowcase was not something I enjoyed, and after five weeks, my skin looked and felt dry.

The minute we arrived back home, I was researching every silk pillowcase brand on the planet to find my replacement. One of the frustrations I had with my old silk pillowcase was that it didn't have a zip, and being silk, it would slip off my pillow during the night. I was googling 'silk pillowcases with a zip', and there were none. *This was my ah-ha! moment.* There it was, right in front of me. *Why don't you just make a silk pillowcase with a zipper,* I said to myself. *How hard can it be?*

This was my next business. From that moment, I started to create a vision for my silk pillowcase brand. I knew a silk pillowcase was a quality product—there's no greater fabric than silk. I knew the Kardashian sisters slept on silk, as like me, they also knew the benefits for your skin and hair. This knowledge also became a strong part of my personal vision for the brand. I envisioned Kim and her sisters wanting to sleep on Shhh Silk. The product that I was going to make was far superior to anything on the market at that time from both an aesthetics and functionality perspective.

This is why your vision needs to be so great and so bold that when you tell people, they think you're crazy. I remember sharing with all of my friends and family that I was creating a silk pillowcase brand and that the Kardashians would sleep on my pillowcases. You can imagine the comments, looks and responses I received. But I didn't let anyone dull my vision. I knew what I was going to create would be something so high quality and beautiful that there was no reason they wouldn't want to sleep on it. More on this later.

I knew that I could make my silk pillowcases more aesthetically appealing than what was currently on the market, and I also had a strong purpose underpinning my brand: to do good.

The 'shhh' in Shhh Silk

This is where the name Shhh Silk comes into the creation of the brand. I called it Shhh Silk for its double meaning. Shhh for quiet and peaceful, after all you spend a third of your life sleeping. But, more importantly, the Shhh represented a secret we would share with our customers after they purchased their silk pillowcase. They would receive a little card with their order that said, 'Shhh ... we've got a secret to share with you. Your purchase today has just helped pay for school supplies for an orphan in Tigray for a year.'

The biggest reason I went with a brand name which, let's face it, is not only hard to say but hard to spell, is because it had meaning and purpose for my vision. This is something I have since learned a lot about. There have been times over the years where business coaches and brand consultants have challenged me to change the name; however, I have stayed true to my initial reasoning and the name has stuck. There was another lesson in this story though: for the first three or four years of growing Shhh Silk, I kept all of the incredible giving we were doing a secret. We would only share it with our customers after they had made a purchase.

A lot of what drove this was from my time spent as a corporate giving sales rep, securing corporate partnerships ranging from $100 000 to $1 000 000 in support of breast cancer research. I witnessed a lot of 'pinkwashing' (using the pink ribbon as a marketing initiative to sell more products, rather than it being about the importance of finding a cure for breast cancer).

While all of the giving we have ever done at Shhh Silk has been driven by the sole objective of doing good, contributing and making a difference, I hadn't realised my own past experiences were holding back my vision to be able to continue doing good. So in 2019, we started talking and sharing more about the incredible giving that our brand has done and continues to do on our website, social media and in interviews. Our brand tagline is: 'Doing good is in our DNA'. We openly ask our customers to hold us true to that promise. Sharing our tagline with our customers in 2020 was the sole driver for us switching all of our products from plastic to an FSC reusable and recyclable paper. Our customers kindly reminded us that doing good includes the planet as well as people.

While I digress a little with this story, I feel it's important to make sure the vision you have for your business is one that excites you and that you are passionate and proud to stand by. You need to be able to dream bigger than perhaps feels comfortable at first, and then you need to be brave enough to stand by this vision, and most importantly, start taking action towards creating this vision. We are going to go into a lot more detail about how you can do this.

This is where passion, mindset and a can-do attitude will serve you well if you want to start a new business. You don't have to wait until you have everything figured out to start. You just need to start. You learn by doing.

Many clients I mentor have great business ideas. Ideas, however, are the easy part. It's committing to getting started that is the real secret to building a business. Let me just repeat that for you. *The secret to creating the life you want or the business you desire is as simple as just starting.* You don't have to start big, you just need to start.

2. Problem-solving skills and an appetite for risk

As a business leader, you need to be able to identify and solve problems effectively and be unafraid to take risks.

I am a solution-focused individual. If you can learn to train your mind to look for solutions to problems, rather than finding more problems, you will start to unlock one of the biggest doors to success. As you work on your business using this book, try to look at your business through a solutions lens rather than finding reasons why something won't work.

LIFE LESSON 4
As Gabrielle Bernstein says, 'become a solution seeker'

When I launched Shhh Silk, I had just over $50 000 in my bank account, which I genuinely thought was more than enough money to launch and grow a silk pillowcase brand. (Spoiler: I was wrong, or at least I made some bad decisions early on with that money.) One of the problems I identified was that I had no budget for marketing. And marketing is crucial for success when you are launching an online business. You can have the best product in the world, but if nobody knows about it, you have no sales.

I had used a large part of my initial savings to invest in stock. I also used a large amount to launch not one, but two Shopify stores. Unlike today, where you can build a website yourself in a matter of hours, in 2015 there were limited options, and websites still required some level of development, which wasn't cheap. The remainder was spent on packaging, inbound freight, customs and a photoshoot. That right there equated pretty close to $50 000.

Damn, how was I going to get anyone to find out about Shhh Silk? Sure, I was spending close to ten hours a day trying to grow and engage our Instagram and Facebook community, but it wasn't enough to generate the sales I would need to keep the business going. I needed to have a big marketing moment, but with zero budget. My first big idea was the one that stuck. I looked at my vision board (yes, I use them, and I believe in their powerful effects) and there were photos of Kim Kardashian carrying her black silk pillowcase through an airport. It looked as though the pillowcase had been handmade, and I truly believed that if I could get some of my silk pillowcases to her, she would love the quality and the hidden zipper.

But how on earth did I plan on doing this? I can hear you asking. Honestly, I didn't really stop long enough to ask myself this question. I truly believed I could make it happen. So I booked a flight to Los Angeles in January 2016 armed with

Kris Jenner's business address. I would hand-deliver some silk pillowcases and a letter telling Kim about my vision to help others as well as more about my life story. (A lot of which you will discover in this book.)

Yes, I took a risk flying halfway across the globe to hand-deliver something that could have easily been express mailed; however, I wanted to make sure I knew the letter and the products had been delivered. I also wanted to show Kim how important it was to me that she received this product as I truly believed she would love it.

Fast forward a few months and Kim's team reached out for some king-size silk pillowcases, and invited us to be involved in a giveaway to her followers via her app (which I will share more about later). There is always going to be a chance that the risks you take don't pay off, but my advice is, isn't it better to try than to not have tried at all? Imagine if I had doubted my idea and listened to everyone who thought the idea of Kim ever using my product was ridiculous. Imagine if I allowed other people's opinions to dull my sparkle. I would have given up on that idea, I would never have taken the risk and I would have missed out on the countless opportunities that Shhh Silk has since experienced with Kim, Khloé, Kourtney, Kylie and Kris.

This story really highlights how, no matter the problem you are facing, there is always a solution. You just need to be brave, have courage and truly back yourself to take a risk and make your own magic happen. Now, a lot has changed since 2016, and I would not turn up on someone's doorstep unannounced to deliver a product; however, that is not to say I wouldn't find an equally as brave and out-of-the-box way of making a first impression with someone for my brand.

The key to taking risks with your business is being okay if some of them don't work. You need to work out your appetite for risk. And, when weighing up the pros and cons, if taking the risk supports your vision, creates more good in the world and drives you to want to succeed, then you are more likely to do whatever it takes to find a solution for your problem. The key is pushing beyond your own fear, taking risks that others are unlikely to take and not stopping long enough to talk yourself out of it. If you believe, even for a split second, that you can do the thing, then you should trust that feeling and take a chance on yourself.

3. Determination and persistence

Starting and growing a business is a challenging process. You need to be determined and persistent in the pursuit of success; have a lot of personal motivation, confidence, discipline; and believe in yourself.

#girlboss?

There are so many perks and benefits to being your own boss. That is one of the reasons why I started both of my businesses. It's also incredibly important for you to be prepared for the other side of business, which is the perseverance and dogged determination it will take to get your business off the ground, and to continue to drive your business forward day by day.

When I started Shhh Silk, I wore the title of #girlboss as a badge of honour. I was completely and utterly sold on the culture that still exists: that to be successful you need to hustle hard and grind, working 18+ hour days. I would regularly glorify photos of myself working at 1 am or 2 am with the hashtag #hustlehard, #gettingitdone or something similar. I can actually feel my body have a physiological response as I reflect on those years. I want to take a moment to reinforce that you *do not need to burn yourself out* to become or be seen as successful.

Sure, you do need to be prepared to work harder than you've likely ever worked before, and have the inner strength and discipline to keep going when you feel like you want to stop. But you also need to know what your boundaries are when it comes to managing your business and your mental, emotional and physical health. Be realistic with yourself about how much time, energy and effort you are able and willing to give to your business, particularly in the first few years. You need a high degree of personal motivation and discipline to continue doing what is required even when you can't see the invisible gains you are making. An image that comes to mind for me that still feels very relatable to the daily struggle is the image of someone trying to push a boulder up a mountain. Where every day you feel like you are putting in an enormous amount of effort and seeing very little to no progress. But little by little, the boulder is moving. There are times where you slip and the boulder rolls back down, but slowly, after a long period of continuous effort, the boulder does make its way to steady ground at the top of the mountain.

The challenge for you will be not knowing how close you are to reaching the top, and whether or not you have what it takes to keep putting in the effort that is required, particularly in the early years. For me, it took close to five years before I even started to feel like the boulder (my business) was reaching steady ground. By this stage, I had suffered many bruises, broken limbs (well not literally, but figuratively) and mental exhaustion on multiple occasions. It felt like I was never going to reach the first flat landing where I didn't have to push so damn hard.

A lot of my personal struggles in pushing my business boulder up the mountain in the early years (much like I did in Joshua Tree in 2022, as shown in figure 3.2) were caused by my financial mismanagement and a lack of budgeting. I didn't display the same discipline in the financial operations of the business as I did in the marketing side of the business. If you want your boulder to reach steady ground sooner than mine did, promise yourself that you will not ignore the financial management side of your business. I will come back to cash flow many times throughout this book, and provide lots of ways in which you can better manage your business cash flow.

Figure 3.2 Olivia pushing a boulder up the canyon in Joshua Tree, December 2022

4. Financial acumen

Understanding financial management and making smart decisions about budgeting, forecasting, pricing and other financial considerations is hands down the most important trait that you need to master when starting and growing your own business. Interestingly, it is also the one that a lot of women struggle with initially, myself included.

Stop avoiding financial management

It's not surprising that many women are still behind men when it comes to understanding finances. The disparity between women and men in understanding finances can be attributed to a combination of historical, cultural and systemic factors; for example, women in Australia could only apply for credit, regardless of their marital status, in the 1970s. Learning to take control and master your understanding of business financial management will take you far in your business. The sooner you understand the financial aspects associated with running a business, the easier it will be for you to make sound financial decisions for your business. Regardless of gender, mastering your understanding of financial management is crucial for success in business.

The first three years of any business are reported as being the hardest. Estimates are that *one in three* new small businesses in Australia fail in their first year of operation, two out of four by the end of the second year, and three out of four by the fifth year. According to a recent study by the University of Technology, Sydney, commonly cited reasons for business failure are, in order of frequency:

- financial mismanagement
- bad management
- poor record-keeping
- sales and marketing problems
- staffing problems
- failure to seek external advice
- general economic conditions
- personal factors.

A closer look at these findings is instructive. *The single largest contributor to business failure is financial mismanagement,* responsible for 32 per cent of all business failures. Contributing factors to financial mismanagement include lack of business experience, cash flow problems, being under-capitalised at the start, excessive private drawings, overuse of credit, having no budget and inadequate provision for tax payments.[3]

Cash flow is the oxygen to your business, and without it, you will end up without a business or, worse still, a business in serious financial difficulty. If you have an ecommerce business and you are struggling financially, there are a few things you should consider when it comes to the financial situation of your business.

The first sign that your business is struggling is if you are failing to pay your bills on time, including rent, wages and taxes. This is a strong indicator that you are experiencing cash flow problems, and you should seek advice from a financial adviser. Ignoring your cash flow problems is never a good idea. You should be as proactive about your business cash position as possible.

LIFE LESSON 5

What losing over $1 000 000 in the first four years of Shhh Silk taught me

When I started Shhh Silk, the first external business I hired, besides a web developer, was a management accountant and bookkeeping company. This allowed me to make sure the business tax obligations, such as monthly reconciliations and business activity statement (BAS) lodgements, were being handled professionally—this is super important.

It took me a few years to understand, however, that a bookkeeper works on the *past* in your business. They review what has been (your month end), and they do not work on the future projections or the performance of your business. I was struggling and so was Shhh Silk. I didn't understand business financial management, I couldn't interpret data from our balance sheet or profit-and-loss statements. I had no real experience managing budgets, even in my role as a general manager. So instead of realising the importance of learning this skill, I ignored my weakness in not understanding margins, business numbers or financial statements for several years, and the business continued to bleed cash and not make a profit.

October 2018 was a pivotal turning point for both me and the business. It was the last time any personal funds were invested into Shhh Silk. Up until this point, my partner at the time and I had invested over $1 500 000 of personal cash into Shhh Silk, and I was still not drawing a wage. It was an absolute mess and a really dark, personally challenging time for me. Something had to change.

If Shhh Silk was to become a sustainable brand, it needed to prove that it could grow without any more investment. It needed professional financial management, something I was not skilled in. So I started to work with Minna, a business service partner, on an annual basis to help me with tax planning and business performance. In 2019, I employed Minna to work with Shhh Silk to focus more on monthly business performance improvement, growth and future planning. It was what the business had needed years earlier.

This is possibly the biggest and most costly mistake I made when starting Shhh Silk.

I should have recognised my own weakness in the area of financial management, and I should have engaged someone sooner to work alongside me, and teach me as the business and I grew together. I remember Minna first reached out to me to offer me this support in year two of Shhh Silk, but I didn't appreciate the value in having these monthly or quarterly meetings and I said no. At the time, I didn't value or understand the benefit this support provides, and how, sometimes, you need to invest money in the right areas, even if they don't seem as sexy as public relations (PR) or marketing. This will help you to not only stop bleeding money, but to have a strong financial plan in place for future growth.

Shhh Silk did not make its first profit until the 2019/2020 financial year. Prior to that, we had four consistent big loss years (equating to well over $1 000 000 of cumulative losses). Even now, having experienced profit year on year for the past three years, the business has still not generated enough combined profit to recover the first four years of losses it experienced.

I really want to be as open and transparent with you as I can be about my business finances in this book in the hope that it helps you to not have to endure the same level of cash flow and financial strain as Shhh Silk has over the years. If you learn one thing from reading this, it's to make sure you have the right support around you to advise you on the best path forward. Someone who can guide you on where you will get the best ROI (return on investment) for your money, and challenge you on where you are overspending money.

I was like a rebellious child with access to money that I didn't know how to handle, and I had no one holding me accountable and no one was guiding me. It's hard to admit this, but Shhh Silk did not need $1 500 000 of personal investment. What it needed was someone who knew what they were doing running the financial side of the business! Once I engaged someone to teach and empower me to understand my business finances and how to manage my business cash flow, Shhh Silk generated its first profit the following year.

At the time of writing this book, Shhh Silk has experienced profit for the past three consecutive financial years, and I was able to start paying myself a salary in 2021. It took me nearly six years of running my business before I finally took control of the financial management and felt empowered to have operating budgets that I understood and respected. I will continue to share more about lessons I have learned around cash flow and personal finance and, more importantly, how I learned to operate our cash flow once we stopped injecting personal funds into the business. Money mindset work and rewriting your money story is a fundamental part of becoming empowered with your finances on your journey to being self-made.

Keeping your finger on the pulse weekly, if not daily, with regards to the financial situation of your business will make a huge difference to the profitability and the overall ease of running your business. You can also read books to educate yourself about financial literacy, listen to business and finance podcasts, join my online community Self-Made Academy or reach out to a business service professional, like I did with Minna, to help you.

I can promise you that ignoring your lack of business financial understanding will only hurt you and your business in the long run.

5. Networking and communication skills

Building a strong network around you is crucial for your success. You need to be an effective communicator and networker, and know how to build relationships with customers, suppliers, partners and investors.

It's not what you know, it's who you know

Networking has always been one of my greatest strengths and something I am going to guide you in throughout this book. Starting a business from home can be isolating, and you can feel extremely alone and disconnected from the bigger community that exists within ecommerce and retail. Now, I studied acting from a very young age, which is likely why networking and building relationships come naturally to me, but it is something that you can learn to master. It's important to connect with people in the industry who have been where you are now and can guide and support you—and even open new doors for you. Some of the networks or events you can look into if you are in ecommerce are retail conferences, and events run by the National Online Retail Association (NORA).

I started attending retail conferences in the first year of starting Shhh Silk, and it has allowed me to get to know a lot of my peers in my industry. I have been invited to speak at many retail events, and I now sit on the Customer Advisory Group for Australia Post, alongside some of the biggest retailers in Australia. I am also proud to be on the Advisory Council at NORA, where I have the privilege of hosting retail events and interviewing people in the online retail network. These opportunities are a direct result of my commitment to and appreciation of networking. Even if you are just starting out in your ecommerce journey, I really encourage you to start developing the confidence to build a network within the industry. The power of personal relationships and their direct correlation to success is something you should never overlook.

If you don't know where to start, joining an online community like Self-Made Academy lets you develop your networking skills in a safe space and build a holistic and truly unique support model for all areas of ecommerce throughout your journey.

6. Adaptability

A strong entrepreneur knows how to adapt to changing circumstances and be quick to pivot when necessary.

A great example of being adaptable is in March 2020 when the COVID-19 pandemic first reached Australian shores. Life as we all knew it was about to change, yet we didn't know how or for how long. This meant every industry in the world needed to adapt its way of doing things. As we saw in Australia, the businesses that adapted quickly managed to survive, or even in some cases, thrive.

In hospitality, it created new innovations like Providoor, which was a meal delivery service allowing restaurant meals to be delivered to your home to support the industry during lockdown. Sadly, Providoor couldn't get the ongoing support it needed post the pandemic lockdowns and announced it was closing in May 2023. Ecommerce in general grew at a rapid rate as people shopped from home. Initially though, as is the case for Shhh Silk where we primarily sell luxury discretionary products like silk pillowcases, sales slowed and then came to a crashing halt all within a three-day period coinciding with the first lockdown in Melbourne in March 2020. I am going to share more detail with you about how we adapted to the slowing demand for discretionary items in Chapter 4. However, I knew we had two choices during this period of rapid change: adapt or die.

It sounds super dramatic when I say it, but that was the honest truth. During that period, we were facing closure of Shhh Silk within six weeks if we didn't change and adapt. So we did. The first thing we did was look at immediate opportunities we could explore. We started to support other female-founded small businesses, and purchased stock from them and sold it on our website. These were items we knew people would spend their money on as they brought comfort during an unsettling time; things such as candles, heat packs, bath salts and other self-care items. We regularly sold out of these items, and were able to continue generating revenue to keep our doors open.

I also started to change the way I was operating our cash flow during this period. This provided me with the wake-up call I needed to change and adapt how I had been running my business. I started to deep dive into financial literacy podcasts and books, and started to teach myself how to manage money and grow wealth. Yes, I know we've already touched on this, but I will continue coming back to cash flow, as I know this will resonate with so many of you, and this will help you to change or adapt how you are running your business.

Some of the initial changes I made to how I was running our cash flow was by managing the business with an operating budget, and sticking to the expense budget as much as possible. I also used a tool called StockTrim to analyse our excess stock (we had close to $1 000 000 RRP in excess stock), and we set up an outlet on our website to start clearing this stock to inject some cash back into the business to invest in face coverings and other fast-moving stock.

I also set up different bank accounts for the business (something I learnt from studying Scott Pape's book *The Barefoot Investor*), and I adapted it to work for the business, putting money into separate accounts (money buckets) for tax, savings, inventory and so on. Operating your business with one account for all incomings and outgoings isn't the smartest way to manage your cash flow. I highly recommend reading Scott's book or researching money buckets, and actioning this for both your business and your personal finances ASAP. This was a game changer for me in learning how to manage money.

At the time of writing this book, the world was recovering from the past few years of the pandemic, facing political issues throughout the world and the after-effect of these events on the global economy. In Australia, in particular, we have experienced monthly interest-rate rises, as well as the cost of rent and food prices increasing. There will always be things happening outside of your business that you cannot control, so it's important to make sure your appetite for constant change and your willingness to adapt is healthy. There will be times where growth in your industry slows or stops altogether; this is when you need to be open to changing as the tides change. If you try to ride the storm without creating a safety net for yourself, it's unlikely you will survive.

A tangible example of how Shhh Silk was able to weather the economic storm was by opening our first physical outlet shop at our head office. We did this in response to the impact economic conditions were having on our customers, and it was important for us to provide options outside of our normal offering. The feedback we have received from customers has been incredible, and it's allowed us to recognise some gaps in the market.

We have now launched an entire category of accessible price point, single-sided silk pillowcases to meet the needs of a lot of our current and new customers. There are always going to be storms you need to weather when running your business, but you need to overcome the natural feeling of being defeated. You need to work out what you *can* do and stop focusing on what isn't working. Be a solution seeker. Just because you launch with one idea or a set range of products, doesn't mean you can't change your plan to meet your needs, the needs of your business and the needs of your customers.

4

How to get started

Launching and building your brand

From idea to launch, it took just over three months for Shhh Silk to be born into the world. I know what you're thinking: how on earth did you build and launch an entire brand in just three months? I had never built a product-based business before, so I had no idea what the benchmark was.

If you are currently working in a job and have a desire to start your own business or leave your job and go all in, there are some important things you need to consider first. In this chapter, I am going to share with you what I did when I started Shhh Silk. But, I will also say, it's not how I would do it today. If you can build your own business with someone else's money (by keeping your job and having a secure income), it will make the early stages more financially manageable and less stressful. If you can make it work, you should try to hold onto your current income as long as possible.

LIFE LESSON 6
Ask yourself how you will pay yourself

It was May 2015 when I jumped from being a full-time employee to a startup founder. I had nothing lined up, no plan and no clue what business I would create next. I had $53 000 in my savings account, and I was about to embark on the trip of a lifetime with my husband at the time and his family to America for five weeks. This trip was a random act of kindness, so generously gifted to us by my ex-husband's parents as a celebration of their hard work, dedication and the success they had both achieved in their careers. My son's grandmother built her own successful service-based business, and she is what I would call the definition of a self-made woman.

There is more to the story behind my quick exit from my job as a general manager than I can share in this book; however, the silver lining was it created an opportunity for me to reassess what I wanted to do in the next chapter of my career. The timing felt right as I would be spending the next five weeks in America, the land of opportunity, and I was sure I would gain some much-needed clarity on what my next move was going to be. I did know one thing for certain, it was time to build my next business.

I was itching to create my second business; I just needed to work through what that was going to be. I had some short-term financial freedom to take the time I needed to work through the next step in my career (or so I thought).

This is an important lesson. Knowing what I know now, eight years on, about the cash required to grow a product-based business, even if I were to do it lean, it's a lot smarter and more financially feasible to build your business while still receiving a stable, secure income from your employer. Truthfully, though, I would not have stayed in my role and built Shhh Silk at the same time. I am an all-or-nothing individual, and it's one of the type A personality behaviours I am still working through with my therapist.

It's my zero-to-a-hundred mindset that has caused me to make some of my biggest mistakes in life and in business. On the flip side, it's also where I've had some of my biggest wins.

The key with taking risks is to find the right balance.

It's okay to start slow

You don't have to leave your job and go all in to start with. Keeping your income will restrict the time you have available, however, the benefit to this is you will have money coming into your bank account, which will likely not happen for a long time when you go all in on your business idea. The brands that are hugely profitable early on are few and far between.

One of the reasons I am so passionate about mentoring women in ecommerce is so I can share openly with them about how normal it is to not be making a profit in the first few years of your business. I didn't know this in 2015, and boy, I wish I did! If I knew how long it would take, I would have likely got a new role and built Shhh Silk on the side. I started Shhh Silk right after the crazy period where Instagram brands who had launched just years prior were literally killing it (or that's how it appeared). Think Aussie brands like Frank Body, Triangl, Showpo and The Daily Edited, who all literally blew up on social media. Paid celebrity endorsements on Instagram weren't even a thing pre-2015. Brands that were early adopters of Instagram were able to amass huge followings on the platform and use that following to boost their growth using the mostly unpaid channel.

By the time Shhh Silk launched in October 2015, it was still so much easier to grow a following organically than it is for a new brand starting on Instagram today. Even then, the days of organically growing a 1 000 000+ following in a matter of months to a year were already starting to come to an end. In the few months leading up to launching Shhh Silk, I had worked tirelessly to grow our Instagram following to over 5000 followers. This definitely helped me to get organic sales online from day one, but it still took years before I started to make profit or pay myself a wage. So, while it's so important to back yourself and take risks, you don't have to go all in if you don't have the financial means to support yourself for an extended period of time.

Taking the first step to start your business can be as simple as registering a business name, researching your idea, setting up your social media profiles or making a phone call to set up a sales meeting with a potential client. Whatever that step is for you, you need to take a leap, back yourself and just start creating your dream. And then you need to commit to taking small daily actions towards your vision.

Commit to taking small daily actions towards your vision.

Would I advise someone to launch a product business in three months? Probably not. However, there is a fine line between too soon and too long when it comes to launching an idea. You need to find your middle ground. Find a timeline that feels like a stretch, but also doesn't create an unhealthy lifestyle of no balance. I had no balance when I launched Shhh Silk; I went all in.

I set up an office in our study at home and spent hours on end researching, designing and setting up my two new websites. I didn't focus on anything else. I was on social media for up to ten hours some days trying to build a following.

Given I was no longer working and had no income coming in, I needed to do whatever it took in the shortest amount of time possible to start earning money again. I promised myself and my husband at the time that I would give myself six months from when I launched Shhh Silk to make online sales, or I would go back to work. I needed to prove that the business would work and that there was a big enough market for silk pillowcases to support a business.

Before you launch your new business and website

I want to share with you a checklist of all of the actions steps you may need to take to start your own business.

Setting up your business

- ☐ Envision your business idea.
- ☐ Decide on your business name.
- ☐ Check that the name is available at asic.gov.au.

- ☐ Check the handle is available on social media.
- ☐ Register a trademark (if required).
- ☐ Work out what products you will sell.
- ☐ Design your products.
- ☐ Do a feasibility study to work out when you might break even.
- ☐ Register your business name.
- ☐ Get business insurance for your products.
- ☐ Work with an accountant to determine the correct structure for your new business and organise an ABN.

Design

- ☐ Hire a freelance graphic designer to create different logo designs; try a platform like freelancer.com or Etsy or if you want to try yourself you can even use a tool like Canva.
- ☐ Organise product and lifestyle photos for your marketing and website.
- ☐ Build a website for around $200, using a good theme on Shopify or similar.

Marketing

- ☐ Create social media accounts for your new business on Instagram, TikTok, Pinterest, Facebook, Threads etc.
- ☐ Create a Google merchant account (google.com/business).
- ☐ Create a Facebook ads account, and teach yourself the dashboard (try the Facebook learning hub).
- ☐ Create a Google Ads account.
- ☐ Do some product market fit research (more on this in Chapter 5).
- ☐ Do some general market research.
- ☐ Register the domain name for your website.
- ☐ Research everything you can about your market, competitors, manufacturing, sourcing, digital marketing etc.
- ☐ Create a brand strategy, you can use artificial intelligence (AI) tools to help you.

- ☐ Create a social media plan.
- ☐ Start posting content on social media to create intrigue, hype and to build an audience.
- ☐ Organise product packaging (preferably sustainable).
- ☐ Organise and design shipping mailing boxes or recyclable satchels.
- ☐ Design a QR code with all of the post-sales information for your customers, like returns, shopping discount codes etc.
- ☐ Make sure all of your Google and Facebook pixels are loaded to the website.
- ☐ Test and launch the website.

Suppliers

- ☐ Research manufacturers (Alibaba can be useful for sampling or initially finding suppliers or attending events such as the Global Sourcing Expo or the Canton Fair).
- ☐ Many retail businesses manufacture their products through China, so if this is you, contact a supplier for an invitation if you plan on visiting your supplier (highly recommended).
- ☐ If you are planning to manufacture in China, don't forget to apply for your Chinese visa.
- ☐ Arrange and finalise samples of your products.
- ☐ Place your first order with your supplier (deposit is usually 30% of the order in USD).
- ☐ Pay the balance of your order to your supplier and wait for the first shipment to arrive.

Sales

- ☐ Work out the pricing strategy for your products. If you are going to wholesale, start with a basic model:
  COST price × 2 × 2.2 = RRP (recommended retail price).
- ☐ Set up Stripe for online payments (stripe.com).
- ☐ Open a business bank account.

- ☐ Set up your accounting software, like Xero.
- ☐ Set up PayPal (paypal.com).
- ☐ Set up Afterpay (afterpay.com) or similar.

Dispatch

- ☐ Set up an account with Australia Post or similar, or investigate using third-party logistics (3PL) who will dispatch your products for you.
- ☐ Buy a thermal printer for your shipping labels, like a Zebra printer.
- ☐ Find a freight forwarder to help you import your goods and help you with customs clearance.

The launch

- ☐ Create a launch plan.
- ☐ Write a press release; a service like Linkby can help you get press from day one (linkby.com).
- ☐ Build a PR gifting list or use services like Tribe or The Right Fit to seed your product for launch.
- ☐ Create a launch strategy for socials.
- ☐ Tell all of your friends and family about the launch and ask them to support you.
- ☐ Finally, celebrate the launch however you feel aligns with your brand!

Next steps: bringing it all together

I am certain I have missed some important steps; however, this list gives you a top-level view of some of the actions required to launch an online brand.

I think it's equally important that I share some of the lessons I learnt from the three months prior to launching Shhh Silk, especially some of the things I would do differently now. The first step is to have a really clear vision for your business so you can build a strong identity around it.

What does your brand look like? Hint: it's more than just a logo

I didn't understand the importance of building a strong brand before launching Shhh Silk. This was evident in the inconsistency in the earlier years of the business, with things like our logo changing three times, our website look and feel changing several times in the first five years, and our packaging changing several times too.

In 2020, I engaged a branding agency to strategically work with the team and me to ensure we knew who we were, what we stood for and how our brand story was being told to our consumers. This is a process I believe should happen *before* your brand is launched, and this was one of the biggest marketing lessons I have experienced with Shhh Silk. The importance of a strongly considered brand is everything. It can be the difference between success and failure with regards to getting your brand off the ground and positioned into the market.

Getting this right in the beginning will make the rest of the brand-building process easier. A branding agency isn't cheap, which is one of the reasons some brands don't use them early on in their journey. A branding agency can cost anywhere from a few thousand dollars to tens of thousands of dollars, so it's important to do your research. If you don't have a large startup cash fund, you can try a platform like Etsy, where at the very least, a freelancer can create a visual brand identity kit for you. This costs a few hundred dollars. It won't include any of the brand strategy work, so you will have to work out a way to factor this into your brand or create it yourself.

AI tools can also be useful in creating some of these documents. Have a play around with prompts around who your brand is and who your ideal customer is, and see if you can develop some brand strategy content to build on. To get you started, you can create some of your own brand strategy by working through these simple steps:

Building your brand story

Once you have decided on the products that you are going to create for your brand, it's important to have a strong brand story. A brand story helps to differentiate you from your competitors. It also allows you to create a connection with your customers on a deeper level.

Here is the Shhh Silk brand story.

Shhh Silk is a brand that believes in the power of better sleep and self-care. Founded in 2015 by Olivia Carr, the company's mission is to provide high-quality silk bedding and accessories that promote comfort and luxury. Shhh Silk's commitment to quality is reflected in its use of the finest materials and its dedication to creating products that help customers sleep better and feel their best.

But Shhh Silk is not just about luxurious products—the company is also committed to doing good and giving back. Through partnerships with organisations and charities, Shhh Silk supports mental health, cancer research, environmental causes, and disaster and emergency relief support. The brand's dedication to social responsibility is reflected in its use of ecofriendly packaging materials and its efforts to minimise its impact on the environment.

Shhh Silk is passionate about creating a better sleep experience and a better world. The company's commitment to quality, comfort and social responsibility has helped it establish a loyal following of customers who appreciate its luxurious and ethical products. With Shhh Silk, customers can enjoy a good night's sleep while also making a positive impact on the world.

The sooner you can design your brand story, the more consistent your brand messaging will be as your business grows.

Grab your notebook and pen as it's time for you to start writing your brand story.

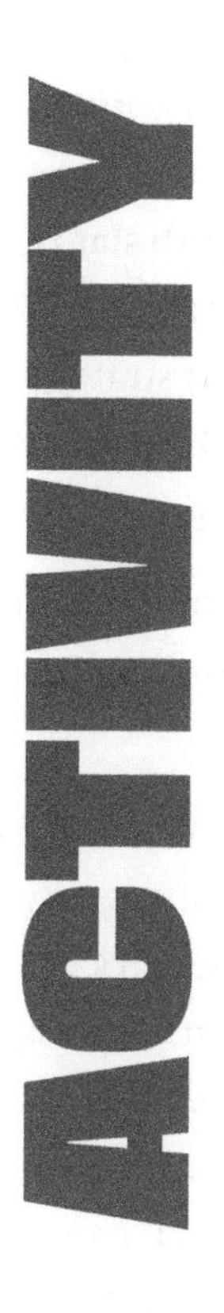

Designing your brand story

Ask yourself the following questions:

- Who is your target audience? Who are you telling your brand story to? What do they care about? What problems do they have?
- What values does your brand stand for? What values are important to you? Why did you start this brand? What difference do you intend to make?
- What is your unique selling proposition (USP)? What sets your brand apart from your competition? Why should customers choose your brand over your competition?

Start to draft a brand story around your values, USP and the difference your brand intends to make.

Read it aloud or record yourself reading it. Does it light you up? Does it excite you? Does it feel aligned to your reason for building this brand?

It's important to remember that your brand story can, and likely will, change and evolve. Without a clear brand story, you are simply selling products and transacting with customers. You want to inspire and connect with your customers so you can create a brand.

Aligning product market fit (which we cover in Chapter 5) with your brand story is so important as it allows you to better understand your target market, learn how to communicate your unique value proposition, and start to build trust and loyalty with your customers. It can also help guide your future product development to better meet the needs of your customers. It is like your north star. Your north star in your business is your long-term business vision. When I started Shhh Silk, I didn't write a business plan or have a polished five-year strategy document. But I did have a very clear north star that has helped to guide and shape my business decisions over the last eight years.

My north star from day one was to support the community, and create quality products that focus on improving people's lives through the power of sleep and self-care.

When building a new business, you can become so overwhelmed by feeling as though you need to have a Fortune 500–worthy mission, vision and values statement. You can over-complicate the process, when really, all you need to do is sit quietly and reflect on what is important to you. Who are you providing your products for? Whose lives are you making easier or more enjoyable as a result of what you are creating? Don't get lost in all of the business lingo that exists, especially if you are building a heart-centred business like Shhh Silk.

One of the most important reasons to go through this process early on in your journey is to stay on course. It can be really easy to lose sight of who you are serving in business and what products they desire. A strong brand story (or north star) will help you see where you are headed and why you are creating these products. Product development becomes easier and more effective when you have a set of rules or guiding principles to follow.

This process also allows you to become customer-centric in your business decision-making. Remember, you are in business to serve your customers, not the other way around.

Develop your brand message

Once you have your brand story, it's time to clarify your brand's purpose, mission and values, and articulate these in a clear and compelling brand message. This message should communicate who you are, what you stand for and what makes your brand unique. Having a strong brand story will make the *why* of your brand clear, which will feed into your mission and vision.

Design your visual identity

Develop a visual identity that reflects your brand's personality and resonates with your target audience. This includes elements such as your logo, colour scheme, typography and imagery. This is where using a freelancer or Canva and Pinterest mood boards can be a cost-effective option to start.

Define your target audience

Identify your ideal customer and create buyer personas that identify their demographics, needs and preferences. This will help you tailor your brand messaging and marketing efforts to effectively reach your target audience. What is their age, gender, education level, income and occupation? What are their shopping habits, interests and hobbies? What are their challenges, problems or frustrations, and how does your product or service solve this?

Create a content strategy

Determine what types of content you will create and how you will distribute it to reach your target audience. This may include social media posts, blog articles, videos or email marketing campaigns.

Build brand awareness

Use various marketing channels to build awareness of your brand and reach your target audience. This may include social media advertising, influencer marketing, search engine optimisation (SEO) or PR. It's important to test these channels to see which ones work best for your brand.

Beyond the brand: logistics

Having a clear brand and a strong brand story is a solid foundation for the rest of your business. However, there are other specific tools and mechanisms you will need to communicate that story, look, feel and emotion to your customers to build connections and generate sales. Each of the following are critical elements that need to be considered, keeping your overarching purpose in mind. Here are some of my tips for tackling the logistics.

Web design

Make sure you understand all of the features you may need for your online store before selecting a pre-made theme on a platform like Shopify. The less customisation or code you require, the cheaper the process will be for you. I decided to create two websites: a '.com.au' for Australia and a second '.com' website for international customers. This is no longer required as a lot of website platforms now allow multiple currencies and international markets on the one website. Running two separate websites comes with a lot of extra work and can also impact your SEO down the track. My tip here is to build the most simple and cost-effective option for yourself from the beginning.

Social media

If you are in a position to outsource your social media content creation and management, this can be a huge time saver. If your brand is primarily online, then spending time creating content, reels, TikToks and so on takes time and commitment. I haven't outsourced the social media management for Shhh Silk, however, over the years we have outsourced content creation from time to time. Automating your content as much as possible is also a huge time saver. Using a scheduling tool, such as Planoly, to schedule your posts will also allow you to have more time and structure in your business. Content will continue to be a huge focus for your brand if you are planning to be online, and automation is your secret weapon. There are so many automation tools you can access to help with content, such as AI tools for captions or content ideas. You can also use tools like Canva to create social media content.

Photoshoots

Photoshoots can become expensive very quickly because you need a location, photographer, models, hair and makeup and so on. If you don't work with a branding agency to create your brand, you also need to work out your own visual direction, and the look and feel for your brand. Everything needs to work together. Your photos need to align with your copy and tone of voice and, importantly, resonate with your consumer. An option to consider is using a content creator from an online service like The Right Fit or Tribe, which will be a less costly exercise than directing your own shoots. You do need to invest in having high-quality product images.

Finding suppliers

Attending importing/exporting expos is a great place to start when you are looking for suppliers. There are also companies such as Sourci that you can partner with that will take care of the entire manufacturing side of the business for you. This would be a good option if you are a one-person business or if outsourcing is important to you. If you want to travel to China, the Canton Fair is a great option as thousands of suppliers attend each year. Alibaba is a useful online platform you can access to start searching for suppliers and testing samples.

Minimum order quantities (MOQ)

This is the minimum per colour or print a supplier will require you to order. Back in 2015, the MOQ for a silk pillowcase was 300 pieces per colour. Over the past few years, with the rise of ecommerce, this has changed. You can now use stock fabric or stock items and customise them to reduce your MOQ, which in turn reduces the initial outlay when placing orders. I would always recommend ordering the lowest possible MOQ to test a product first. The usual terms in China for payment are 30/70: 30% deposit when placing your order and 70% when the goods are ready to ship.

Currency

Another factor to consider when manufacturing your product overseas is that you will likely be charged in US currency. If you are selling your products in Australian currency, you will need to work out the conversion when setting your prices. Currencies fluctuate, so make sure to take this into consideration. You also pay customs on the converted amount in Australian dollars when your product lands in Australia.

Packaging

Getting your visual identity worked out before you create your packaging will also save you money in the long run. Important things to consider are choosing the smallest and lightest possible options to save you money on postage, but also to save waste. Make sure the options you choose are as environmentally friendly as possible. Sustainability should be a big focus for any business owner.

Third-party logistics (3PL)

I used my home office as my warehouse when I launched Shhh Silk. A more sustainable option for growth may be looking into a 3PL partner. A 3PL will store and ship your inventory for you, which means you don't need to handle the logistics of shipping orders and can focus on growing your business. Shhh Silk offers personalised products so we can't use a 3PL provider. This is something to consider when you are scaling: can you use a 3PL in other countries, or does something have to happen to your product beforehand, like customisation?

Marketing

If you plan to launch an online business or you are planning to grow your online business, you will need to generate some cash flow or have available capital to use digital marketing channels, such as Facebook, Google and TikTok. I invested over $200 000 in digital marketing in the first year of Shhh Silk without any experience in creating or scaling ads. This meant I didn't generate a positive return. You can lose a lot of money through digital marketing if you do not educate yourself or seek a partner to help you with digital advertising.

The average return-on-ad spend (ROAS) is usually somewhere around 3x. So, on average, for every $100 you spend, you should be generating at least $300 in revenue. This is an average, as on some platforms you will be able to generate a much higher ROAS. There are courses you can enrol in or you can teach yourself how to use social media ads.

Over the years, I have worked with many different marketing agencies on our digital advertising, and also educated myself on the basics of Google and Facebook. As these platforms are ever-changing, it is good practice to take ownership of this and learn the basics until you can comfortably afford to hire someone to do it for you. Eight years in and I still regularly upskill myself on digital marketing.

Digital marketing is just one of the many ways in which you can create revenue for your business. Just like your P&L, you need to monitor your Facebook dashboard daily to make sure you are generating a positive return on your ad spend. My observation working with many ecommerce brands is that there is no one-size-fits-all approach to digital marketing. What works for one brand, may not work for yours and vice versa. Test and review your marketing channels regularly.

PR and content creator (influencer) gifting

People will have different views on the importance of these two things. The majority of brands in a growth phase will tell you they are crucial. Bill Gates is, somewhat controversially, believed to have said, 'If I was down to my last dollar, I would spend it on PR.'

The cheapest form of marketing when you are growing is to gift your product. Back in 2015, it used to be to macro/large influencers that brands would gift to (and you can read more on how we did this with the Kardashians in Chapter 15); however, this has changed to focus on micro influencers. There are several different platforms you can use, such as #Giftly, Tribe or The Right Fit, to make your product gifting easier.

You should never look at gifting as sending free products, but rather view it as placing your best-selling, hero products in the hands of the right people to get your product seen by as many potential customers as possible. If you look at the cost of your product, this is a cheap form of marketing. The key is to gift regularly, choose content creators who align with your brand and make sure their audience is a fit with your ideal customer.

When it comes to PR, this is usually handled through an agency. Their fee structure will be a monthly retainer, usually anywhere between $3000 and $5000, depending on the services required. If you don't have the budget to use a PR agency, you can use platforms such as Linkby for what is called pay per click marketing. You essentially write your own media release or press release (you can use an AI tool to help you), and publish it to their platform. You can select the publications to pitch it to, such as *Vogue, Daily Mail* etc. If the media outlet accepts your article, they will publish your article and will charge you a fee, anywhere from $1.50 upwards for every click you receive on the article. The campaign budget is usually around $2000 to $5000 per article so you can control the spend per click. This is a great way to get 'as seen in' type PR for your brand. In my experience, you don't usually get enough clicks to use the whole budget, so you don't need to have $5000 for every article you publish. The better the article, the better the result.

This is also a little intel into how some brands create 'hype' for their products. Ever seen articles such as 'Brand X sold out because so and so were spotted wearing their product'? You can create your own articles, and you control the narrative. It's also a friendly reminder not to believe everything you read online about other brands (wink, wink). See, comparison is dangerous as you may be comparing your brand to hyped brand building content, rather than the actual profitability or performance of another brand. There is nothing wrong with hyping your brand—it can be a powerful marketing strategy—just don't waste time comparing yourself to other brands.

Overall, the most important advice I can give you when thinking about starting a new business—besides to just start—is to factor in all of the elements of building a brand we have discussed here. *There is so much more to building your brand than just creating your beautiful product.* While I have highlighted a lot of the different elements needed to create a new business, there are always new things that come up, and a lot of them you will learn and figure out along the way. But the only way you will be able to know if your idea is a good one is to take the first step towards starting your business. Regardless of how much planning you do, some things will work and some things won't. This is part of running a business.

Most women I work with say they just don't know where to start. That is fair, but my advice is this: *start by taking consistent action every day*. For you, that might mean researching or creating a mood board. It doesn't matter where you start, you just need to start.

What I didn't understand when I first launched Shhh Silk, was how to read a profit-and-loss statement or a balance sheet or how to create a forecast or budget. The numbers side of running a business would be a big problem down the track, and you will hear more about this in the following chapters.

5

Product market fit

A prerequisite for sustainable cash flow and profitability

One of the most important factors in running a successful and profitable business is cash flow management; a close second is product market fit. How well you manage your cash flow will have a significant impact on the profitability and longevity of your business.

Cash flow can also be the most challenging and stressful part of running your own business. And depending on your prior experience when it comes to running a business, you will learn most of the important financial management principles by doing.

The better you are at handling your own personal finances and budget, the easier you will find managing your business cash flow.

Nearly every woman I have ever mentored in business has said that cash flow is their biggest challenge. This is closely followed by understanding financial metrics and being able to read and interpret their profit-and-loss statement (if they even have one).

Business success really can be summed up in the formula:

INCOME – EXPENSES = PROFIT

Making sure you are generating more income than you are spending is the most basic fundamental principle of owning a profitable business.

Where this formula is too basic is in the early stages of starting or growing a business, as it takes time for income to grow. Starting from a $0 base for income sets you behind in the early stages while you have expenses to cover. One of the lessons I want to share with you (that I learned the hard way) is how important it is for you to do a feasibility exercise on your new business before you start, or if you have started, before you get too deep into investing your personal funds. Most women I have worked with who start their own business don't have a strong understanding of the financial management side of running a business—and I didn't either. This can translate into a lack of understanding of how to do a feasibility study on their new business idea.

I am going to give you some tips on how you can make this an easy and enjoyable process. Technology has come a long way since I started Shhh Silk in 2015, and thanks to powerful tools like AI technology and ChatGPT, you are better equipped now as a business owner than ever before. You can use technology to help you understand and build financial models. It's so important to understand the reality of how much money you are going to need to invest and generate in your first few years to grow your business. The better equipped you are from the very beginning, the more strategic you can be with your decision-making and how you launch and operate your new business.

A recent study of 300 Shopify store owners in the USA[4] found that small business owners spend an average of $40 000 on expenses in their first full year of business. It also noted that you shouldn't expect to make a profit in the first 24 months of business.

Now this is where it can get even trickier to predict how long it will take for your business to make a profit. There are so many factors involved when it comes to how quickly a business can make a profit. One of those important factors is *product market fit*. One of the crucial elements of business success that I wish I had considered more seriously before launching Shhh Silk, is the concept of product market fit or market demand.

What is product market fit?

The Lean Startup book by Eric Ries summarises the definition of product market fit as: 'the moment when a startup finally finds a widespread set of customers that resonate with its product'.

Having a strong product market fit is critical for business success as it means there is demand for your product.

In an article published by Shopify, Eric Even Haim, CEO of up-sell and cross-sell app ReConvert, shared that you need to create or sell an amazing product with proven market demand.[5] Take a look at the top retailers today—Allbirds, hellotushy.com, Bombas—and you'll notice they all sell top-tier products.

Eric says, 'Product quality is critical because a good product sells itself...When you marry a great product with an audience who's hungry for it, your marketing becomes 10 times easier.' In fact, new products don't have to be the 'next big thing'. You just need to 'look for growing trends and markets where customers are underserved. Then step in with an excellent product and give them what they want!'

Two places to find market demand are:

- Google Trends (trends.google.com), where you research the popularity of topics people search for.
- Trends.co, which uses data to predict trends and business opportunities before they become popular.

While we have always offered great quality products at Shhh Silk, we also sell a very niche product. When we started, there were only a handful of brands globally that sold pure silk pillowcases. Fast forward to 2023, and there are more than 100 silk pillowcase brands serving a relatively small market.

I would also say the market wasn't hungry enough for silk pillowcases in 2015. I went in a little early. This meant a lot of marketing effort and investment were required in the early years to educate consumers about the benefits of switching to a silk pillowcase. However, as our business has grown, along with our competitors and our combined marketing efforts, so has the demand for silk pillowcases (see figure 5.1).

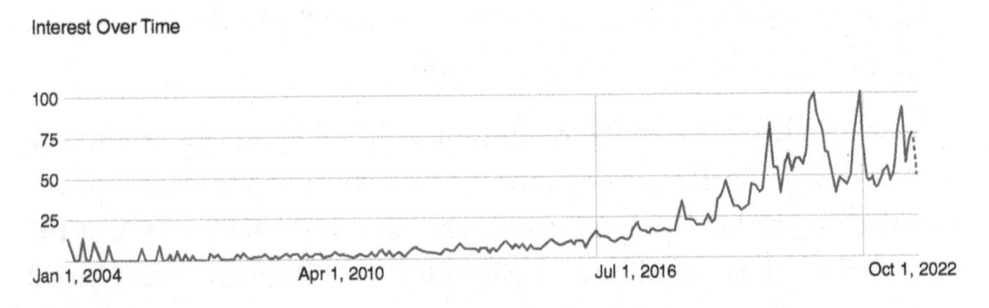

Figure 5.1 worldwide silk pillowcase trend from 2004

If I were launching an ecommerce brand today, I would start with a quality product that already has proven market demand and a much broader audience. Niche products can and do work well, so long as there is strong demand. Being first to market requires more investment to educate consumers about your products.

The easiest way to find out if there is an appetite for your product is by using a tool like Google Trends. For example, if you are passionate about launching a product in the apparel industry, you would search by 'apparel' and you may apply a filter for Australia, depending on your shipping and distribution plans. You can apply filters for the time period you want to look at and see if there are certain search terms being used a lot. This can help you to see if the product you are planning to launch has a high demand.

Don't find customers for your product, find products for your customers.

Let's explore this idea together now. Grab your notebook and pen:

ACTIVITY

Analysing your industry trends

Experiment with Google Trends, adding in keywords and applying filters. Answer the following questions in relation to your brand.

- What is the product or idea you are thinking about launching?
- What is the current trend for the product or service?
- Is the demand for your product growing or declining?
- Are there other products related to your offerings that are in demand?

- Can you use this data to drive new product ideas for your business?
- If the demand isn't there for your product, do you have the funds required to educate your customer and create demand?
- Are you open to exploring new products or ideas based on greater demand or trends?
- If you are entering a market with a product that is in high demand, what is your point of difference?
- How will your products stand out?

By examining the trends that are affecting your industry, you get a much longer-term view to consider when planning and deciding where to invest your funds. You also have an evidence base to fall back on when making these decisions.

LIFE LESSON 7
Doing your research and getting your product off the ground

For me, the process of starting Shhh Silk was flying to China three days after having the idea of starting the business. See, there's my zero-to-a-hundred attitude in overdrive again. You don't need to jump on a plane to China. If you are planning to build relationships in this region, you should start learning about manufacturing;

Chinese business culture; and the process of negotiating pricing, making samples or getting prototypes made.

I was optimistic, but realistic when I made the decision to explore the idea of this business. What I failed to do, though, was any sort of financial modelling, forecasting or budgeting—please don't make the same mistake. This one step can save you a lot of money and unnecessary stress in the future. Now, I realise projections and forecasts are not actual and there are always unknowns; however, you will still have a better understanding of what you are dealing with financially.

So with my savings and a clear vision in my mind of the business I was going to build, I agreed to give myself a six-month timeline to test whether it was just me who was obsessed with sleeping on a silk pillowcase, with a hidden zipper, or whether strangers on the internet wanted one too.

So I jetted off to Shanghai for the first of many trips to China. I didn't, and still don't, speak more than a few words of Mandarin. I knew absolutely nothing about manufacturing products in China or about importing, but I was naive, inspired, excited, curious and keen to learn. I do think a healthy level of naivety is important when you are starting a new business (just not when it comes to finances).

If you are looking to start a product-based business and you are planning to import products from China, my advice is to visit the factories you are working with.

Not only is it important to check the working conditions in the factory, it is a very important step of the relationship- and trust-building process, both critical factors in Chinese culture. Your suppliers will become your business partners, and in order to have a smooth, high-quality production process, you need to build a strong relationship with your suppliers.

Always insist on visiting the manufacturing factory, not just the sales office. This is an important step in your quality control process. I have also found it to be the easiest and fastest way to produce new product samples.

If you haven't found a supplier yet, or you are struggling to wrap your head around who to work with, another great idea is to visit the Canton Fair, also known as the China Import and Export Fair, which usually takes place in April each year and is one of the largest trade fairs in the world. The event typically attracts over 25 000 exhibitors and around 200 000 buyers from more than 210 countries and regions. It's a fabulous way to find new suppliers for your brand. You will need to allocate a few days to get the most out of your time at the fair.

In my opinion you don't need to spend more than four or five days at a time in China, depending on how many products you are working on, as the manufacturers are incredibly hard-working people and a lot happens very quickly. Just be prepared and maximise your time.

I returned from China with nothing more than a sample of a pink silk sleep bonnet, a black silk pillowcase and a white silk pillowcase from the different factories I visited. But I knew this was all I needed to launch Shhh Silk.

I made sure I had a better quality product than what already existed on the market. Shhh Silk was the first to introduce a hidden zipper to our silk pillowcases, ensuring they stayed put while you slept. This added cost to the product, however, it also made our pillowcase superior to what was already on the market and created a better experience for the consumer. I also chose to create aesthetically on-trend patterns for our range as opposed to the plain colours that were being offered by our competitors at the time. And thirdly, and possibly most importantly, I launched with a strong purpose behind the brand, giving back from day one. (I will touch more on this later.) This allowed Shhh Silk to not only have a point of difference in our product offering, but I was able to start to build a brand story, and not just sell a product.

6

How to manage your business cash flow

From chaos to control

Most people will use their own savings to start a business and, in my experience, they often underestimate how much cash is required to get a business off the ground. If you are creating your own products, as opposed to drop shipping (products you ship direct from a supplier, and you don't hold any stock for), this will likely require a lot of capital or personal cash injections to manufacture your product (and pay for it up front).

It's so important to have a strong understanding of financial management before diving head first into building your product-based business. If you don't get the numbers and your cash flow right, it can end up being a very costly lesson. Before you do anything in your new business, run your numbers, and work out how much cash you will likely need. If you don't know how to do this, you should see a financial expert who can help you work through your initial cash flow projections and create a feasibility study for you. Getting these things right from the start will save you money in the long run.

As you will discover in this chapter, if you don't have an operating budget or a financial plan for how you will grow your business, you face the real possibility of losing your money or, worse still, your business.

LIFE LESSON 8
Do I really need investors and can I manage their investment?

I quickly realised my savings weren't going to be enough to get Shhh Silk off the ground. I had no prior experience in raising capital so I decided to share my business ideas with my previous boss to see if he would be interested in investing. At first, he seemed reluctant and didn't think I had enough SKUs (stock keeping units or individual products) to build a profitable business online. He works for a large Australian retailer where he was used to brands selling thousands of different items online, not just the initial four I was launching.

He asked me if I really thought I could generate over a million dollars in revenue from silk pillowcases. I told him, absolutely, I could. After considering the idea, he decided he loved my passion and enthusiasm and agreed to invest. I used that money to retain a PR firm in America (approximately US$5000 a month), for the two of us to travel to America to take part in the Golden Globes gift lounge, and the rest to start some Facebook ads.

The PR firm also required stock every month for influencer and celebrity gifting, so I decided to purchase more stock, and within a matter of months, the investment was gone. I had an unhealthy mindset and motto when I launched Shhh Silk, which was 'invest to grow'. What that meant was I was telling myself daily that, in order to grow, I needed to continue pumping enormous amounts of cash into the business—which a lot of businesses do. However, there are two main differences here: 1) I didn't have enormous amounts of cash or a private equity firm funding my growth, and 2) I had no operating budget, so there was no structure or strategy to where I was investing the money. This was a big and expensive lesson.

Over the first three years, my partner and I would reinvest every dollar generated from Shhh Silk back into the business, as well as inject a further $700 000 of additional cash into Shhh Silk. Combined, we both invested over $1 500 000 of cash into Shhh Silk in the first three years of operating.

This was a huge mistake.

Investing to grow was my mask for the truth that I had no idea how to manage cash flow, didn't understand the fundamentals of the business financials, and didn't know what it took to manage the finances behind running a business—or even create an operating budget. Instead, I continued to throw money into digital advertising, PR and digital agencies; purchase more stock; lease an overpriced nine-person office; and employ a team before the business was ready.

To say I was in over my head is an understatement. I was churning through money faster than it was being generated. I hadn't yet worked out how to operate the business without requiring more and more money. I was so hyper focused on top-line growth (revenue growth) that I was completely ignoring the bottom line (profit). Even though by year three we had our first ever seven-figure year, I knew something was seriously wrong. We still weren't making a profit and there was no external cash left to invest. I was spending too much money on growing the revenue of the business and I was also spending it in the wrong areas.

There's a simple equation in accounting: *spend less than you earn.*

Time to make some changes

I had to make some serious changes to how I had was running the business. I needed to start cutting my expenses significantly if Shhh Silk was to survive. I had to start over.

I downsized the team, closed the PR firm I had started (a story for another book) and looked for a commercial warehouse where the lease would be half of the price we were currently paying.

But this was only the beginning. I knew I would also need to start educating myself on the financial side of running a business. I needed to start enjoying numbers and stop ignoring them. Luckily, by this stage, the business was making decent revenue even if it wasn't yet making profit, so I knew I had a choice: change everything or lose everything.

At this point, I also started to experience mental health issues, more specifically, anxiety and high stress. I was no longer enjoying going into the office every day, and I was beginning to resent my business. I had unknowingly started to attach my own self-worth to the success, or lack thereof, of the business. I wasn't paying myself a wage, and I was solely reliant on my partner, which was starting to eat away at my sense of self and independence. I felt I couldn't talk to anyone about what I was really going through as I was operating the business from an ego mindset, and I didn't want anyone to know how badly I and the business were struggling. I felt like a complete failure.

I started working with a spiritual coach and a kinesiologist to guide me on my journey of inner self discovery. I am thankful I started my deep inner healing journey, and this is a journey I am still on today.

Inner work is really just another form of self-development, although perhaps it's a more personalised approach to self-development. Gabrielle Bernstein, on her 2023 tour of Australia, made a good point when she said we need to think of another way to describe it than 'work'. I guess one of the terms I would use to describe it is 'self-prioritisation' or 'committing to self'. This work really was the start of me building the mindset and self-belief I needed to turn the financial success of Shhh Silk around and go on to make a profit, start to repay my ex-partner some of his initial investment back, pay myself a salary and start to build my personal wealth. I'm going to walk you through my journey of inner healing work in Chapter 7.

Reflection and hindsight are wonderful things. They are how I have continued to learn and grow. I have made a number of mistakes in my life, but I have viewed all of them as lessons to push me forward towards a more successful and bigger life. They are also what I use as lessons in this book, to allow you to grow and learn without having to live the same challenging experiences I have.

I am now an advocate for self-funded founders to focus on the bottom line first to build a profitable business, rather than, like me, getting caught up in the comparison trap of what businesses online are making, and then focusing on the revenue growth of your business rather than making actual money. It is crucial for you to have money in the bank to sustain and grow a business if you don't have access to funding.

Sole trader vs company

Another lesson I wish I had known sooner was that, in order for me to be able to repay myself the cash I invested into my business when I started, I should have set Shhh Silk up as a company not as a sole trader (seek your own expert advice with this). This would have allowed me to allocate all of my personal cash contributions as a loan to the business that the business would one day need to repay me (tax-free).

The majority of the money my ex-partner and I invested into Shhh Silk was prior to me setting the business up as a company, which means we wouldn't get that money back if I were to sell the business. It's important for you to seek advice on this, as the most likely time you will invest your own cash into the business is at the beginning, when the business needs cash. While you don't get this money back if you are a sole trader, you do, however, get to carry forward your personal losses when you do your personal tax return. My advice is to speak to your accountant about this and ask what would be best for you if you are planning to set up a business.

If you haven't started your business yet and want to do a basic exercise to determine how much cash you will need to start your business, you can do a really simple exercise called a startup cost analysis.

ACTIVITY

Startup cost analysis

Make a list of all the expenses you will need to cover before you start generating revenue. This can include things like website design and development, inventory, shipping materials, marketing expenses, legal and accounting fees, and any other startup costs.

Estimate the cost of each item on your list. Do some research to get accurate estimates for each expense, and be sure to include any taxes or fees.

Add up the estimated costs to get a total startup cost. This will give you an idea of how much cash you will need to start your ecommerce business. It's always wise to add a buffer in to cover those unexpected costs that will crop up!

Determine how you will finance your startup costs. Will you use personal savings, take out a loan or seek out investors? Make a plan for how you will fund your startup costs and ensure that you have enough cash to cover them.

Monitor your expenses and adjust your budget as needed. As you start your ecommerce business, keep track of your expenses and make adjustments to your budget to ensure that you stay on track financially.

It is important to keep in mind that your startup cost analysis is a very rough estimate, and that your actual costs may vary. However, by doing this analysis, you will be better equipped to make informed decisions about your new business and how to manage your initial finances effectively.

After completing your startup cost analysis, the next step is to create a budget and determine how you will actually finance your business.

Creating a budget

Use the numbers from your startup cost analysis to create a simple budget for your business. This budget should include all of your anticipated expenses, such as rent, utilities, equipment, inventory, marketing and salaries. Be sure to include both fixed and variable expenses.

Fixed expenses are costs that remain the same each month, regardless of your revenue, such as rent, salaries, insurance and equipment. Variable expenses, on the other hand, are costs that fluctuate based on your revenue, such as shipping, marketing, Shopify transaction fees etc.

Determine your funding sources

Decide how you will fund your business. This may include your personal savings, a business or personal loan, crowdfunding or investors. Research your options and choose the best financing option for your business.

Track your expenses

When you start your business, it's important to track your expenses often and compare them to your budget. This will help you identify areas where you may need to cut costs or adjust your budget. You can run this on an Excel or Google sheet to start with, or better still, an accounting system like Xero. If you are like me and prefer the sales and marketing side, this is often the really boring side of running a business, but it is, honestly, the most important part. You need to manage the financial side of your business or have someone help you from the beginning who is managing a budget, not just reconciling your bank account. You need to watch every dollar. You need to make sure you are making more than you are spending.

Revise your budget

If you find that your actual expenses differ from your projected budget, revise your budget often or as necessary. This will help you stay on track financially and make informed decisions about your business. I started using an operation budget in year six of Shhh Silk. If I started from year one, things would have likely turned around faster than they did from a profitability perspective.

Seek advice

Consider seeking advice from a financial adviser or an accountant to help you manage your finances and make informed decisions about your business. This is something you should budget for, as it will help you manage your business more efficiently from the onset.

By creating a budget and working out where you will find the cash to support your business, you can launch your business with a solid financial plan. Tracking your expenses and revising your budget as necessary will help you stay on track and make informed decisions.

Every business will require a different level of cash to get it off the ground. Do I think you need seven figures to start, grow and build a product-based business like I did? Absolutely not. The real lesson in this chapter is that the more educated and confident you can be in *how* to manage cash flow and control expenses in your business and the more you focus on *profit* not just revenue, the more successful your business will be.

7

Business success and fulfilment

What's love got to do with it?

The four-letter L word. You may wonder, what does love have to do with building your business or becoming self-made? Honestly, everything. In the words of Brené Brown, 'Owning our story and loving ourselves through that process is the bravest thing we'll ever do.'

For years, I have asked myself, 'What is love?' If I were to ask you to answer that question right now, you would have a very different response to me, or anyone else for that matter.

After years of self-healing and inner work, I now believe that *love is not one thing; it is everything.*

And that love starts with self-love.

Love is how you create meaning in your work; interact with others; build your business; set boundaries; spread kindness to others; mentor your team; take action towards your own goals; and even choose to spend your money. It is, of course, more complex and multi-dimensional than this, and doesn't need to be broken down further in this book for you to be able to understand the role self-love plays in building your business and helping you achieve greater success in your life. How it can help you become self-made.

Sometimes though, it can be easier to identify what something is not. Grab your pen and notebook—it's time for some honest reflection on how much self-love you are cultivating in your life and in your business right now.

ACTIVITY

What does self-love look like for you?

Tick all of the boxes that resonate with you about how you are currently running your business—even if you are operating your business as a solo operator.

In my business, I:

Ineffective	Effective
☐ feel like an imposter	☐ feel confident
☐ have self-doubt	☐ set boundaries
☐ feel overwhelmed	☐ work on my resilience
☐ am burnt out	☐ am a confident leader
☐ struggle with communication	☐ am comfortable with decision-making
☐ micro-manage my team	☐ am creative

- ☐ feel insecure
- ☐ avoid difficult conversations
- ☐ neglect self-care
- ☐ avoid delegating tasks
- ☐ build a positive work culture
- ☐ promote innovation
- ☐ view setbacks as opportunities
- ☐ take risks

Which of these lists has the most ticks for you? Are you tracking in a healthy self-love, self-made place with your business? Or has this highlighted a few areas you could work on to enhance your self-love within your business?

Remember, developing self-love is a process, and it takes time and practice. By incorporating more self-love practices into your daily life, you can begin to cultivate a deeper sense of self-love and acceptance.

If your list was a bit lacking on the self-love side, here are some simple, cost-effective practices you can incorporate into your daily routine:

- Write down five things you love about yourself every day.
- Practice a form of exercise that you enjoy, such as dancing, hiking or yoga.
- Take a relaxing bath or shower and treat yourself to a favourite body wash or bath bomb.
- Practice mindful breathing exercises or meditation to centre yourself and calm your mind.

- Treat yourself to a favourite healthy snack or meal that nourishes your body. (For me, that's Loco Love chocolates! What a pleasurable moment.)
- Spend time in nature, such as going for a walk in a local park, heading down to the beach or hiking in the mountains.
- Spend time doing something creative that brings you joy, such as painting, drawing or playing music.
- Take a break from social media and spend time connecting with friends and loved ones in person or over the phone.
- Read a book or watch a favourite movie that inspires and uplifts you.
- Practice positive affirmations, such as telling yourself, 'I am worthy and deserving of love' or 'I am enough just as I am'.

Prior to experiencing burnout and beginning my self-healing work, I could easily have ticked all of the boxes in the left-hand column. I didn't set boundaries with my team, I avoided the difficult but necessary conversations, and I micro-managed. These are not great qualities in a leader. A book that is brilliant for learning to develop more self-love is Jay Shetty's *8 Rules of Love*.

There is a saying that I often refer to: how you do one thing is how you do all things.

LIFE LESSON 9
Developing self-love

From as young as I can remember, I was told by my father that 'children should be seen and not heard'. For anyone 40 or older, this may sound all too familiar. I did some research to find out exactly where this saying comes from and the context behind it. Multiple sources attribute the phrase to *Mirk's Festial: Collection of Homilies*, by John Mirk, an Augustinian clergyman, circa 1450.[6]

After some reading on this topic, my interpretation of this now very outdated saying is that it was originally used to silence and control young children, to communicate that their thoughts were not important, and it was aimed in particular towards young women.

I find it fascinating that phrases like this can continue to carry such weight so many years after they appeared in print.

I, of course, had no idea of the origin of this phrase when I was growing up, but I know I never felt worthy when hearing it said to me by my father. Another phrase I would often hear throughout my childhood and into my late teens was 'stop showing off'. Even if what I was sharing was an accomplishment, I would be told to stop showing off and would be made to feel small. These examples were not the only root causes of my lack of self-love or self-worth, but they raise a good point. Our childhood conditioning and upbringing do have a significant role to play in our development of self-love and self-esteem.

My childhood home environment was sadly not one filled with love. I experienced the damaging effects of my father's alcoholism, abuse and control. I didn't experience any positive modelling from my parents on how to give or receive love in relationships. It wasn't until years later when I started doing some self-healing work that I recognised the damage to my self-esteem, and could see the lack of self-love stemming from my childhood and the environment in which I was raised. I have struggled with intimate relationships, developing trust, and even feeling as though I have never truly loved a partner. I have learnt to build walls and wear an invisible suit of armour to feel protected and not allow myself to feel pain or uncertainty. I realise now that, while I thought I was protecting myself by doing this, all I was actually doing was not allowing myself to be vulnerable, open or seen, which is a block to experiencing love and joy.

I'm sharing how my lack of self-love has played out in my life both personally and professionally to remind you that how you do one thing is how you do all things.

In her book *Daring Greatly*, Brené Brown describes vulnerability as 'uncertainty, risk, and emotional exposure'. It's the unstable feeling we get when we step out of our comfort zone or do something that forces us to relinquish control. She also describes vulnerability as doing something even though you can't control the outcome.

I used to believe I was good at being vulnerable. I am such an open book and I share a lot of my life on social media, on stage at my keynotes or online via my blog posts. I was fascinated when I discovered that sharing is not the same as being vulnerable. I realised that every time I share, including in this book, I am still in control of what I share and how much I share (I still have my suit of armour on).

Again, Brené Brown shares, 'vulnerability is the birthplace of love, belonging and joy'.

When I was in my early 30s, I witnessed my mother being vulnerable for the first time. She showed immense courage and bravery and decided to leave my father after 35 years of marriage and abuse. She took a huge risk, filled with so much uncertainty around her future, shelter, emotional wellbeing, financial stability, not to mention a lot of emotional exposure. Now at the time this was happening, I wasn't aware enough to see this as my mother being vulnerable. In truth, I held a lot of confusion and resentment towards my mum for years after that, wondering why she hadn't done it sooner, and removed my sister and me from the abusive environment. Thankfully, with the help of a spiritual coach and a psychologist, I was able to move through those feelings and come to appreciate and understand just how brave and courageous my mother was.

Your past is not your present

I had my first boyfriend when I was 13. Since then, I've had 28 years of dating and relationships. The biggest thing I have come to learn about childhood trauma through my years of therapy is that we keep repeating the patterns or cycles of behaviour until we learn the lesson. The lesson for me has always been to allow myself to have an open heart and be vulnerable. Growing up, I never witnessed my father be vulnerable until years later when he moved into aged care and became completely reliant on others due to his Alzheimer's disease.

I have been engaged four times, married once and divorced within my first year of marriage. Ironically, I have been single for the entirety of writing this book, and it's also the longest period of time in my life that I have chosen to spend some quality time in solitude getting to truly know myself, love myself and further work on my blind spots. Just as you may be learning about yourself and your business by reading this book, I have also learnt so much about myself writing this book. I am excited to start dating again in the future, and it will be the first time I get to really show up, allow myself to be seen, remove my armour when I feel ready, and be vulnerable and brave. This is a huge growth moment for me, and is the direct result of working on myself and my commitment to developing more self-love.

When I started writing this chapter, I wrote about how closed off I was to love. I shared this with my therapist, and he has been helping me work to remove my use of absolute language, and change my all-or-nothing thinking patterns that play out in both my personal and professional life. Once you start doing some inner work on yourself, you will see some common threads and start to understand how your patterns are all intertwined.

All-or-nothing thinking is usually a common perfectionist characteristic, and can also be experienced by people with mental health conditions such as anxiety. All-or-nothing thinking generally means you think there are only two options: success or failure. So, again, instead of being vulnerable and taking risks, I would use this pattern of behaviour as a coping mechanism. I can share this as I know I am not broken and there is nothing wrong with me; however, I know my current patterns and thinking styles around love are not serving me as I want to experience more love, joy and belonging in my life. Developing more self-love and self-worth is a choice. And just like building a business, it takes work, daily action and commitment. It's a journey, not a destination.

Learning to prioritise your own needs and emotional health can help you to become more resilient and to better manage the challenges that arise in your personal and professional life.

When I look back at how I was ignoring my debt in my early 20s, I am now able to see (after years of therapy and inner work) that a lot of these behaviours stemmed back to my lack of self-worth and self-love, and my internal belief systems. The more work I have done over the years on my self-worth, the more I value simple things like a clean car, clean clothes, personal hygiene, a well-made bed, exercise and a tidy house. You will notice none of these things cost money. They are things that make me feel better about myself and my life.

The better I became at mastering self-discipline, the more disciplined I was with my business. I may not have had the experience with business finances in the early years, but I did develop the self-discipline required to keep moving forward when it felt like I was never going to finally get that boulder to the top of the hill. I had the self-discipline to seek more help, get honest with myself about my ego, and do the ongoing work required to become self-made and build a big life for myself.

The overall lesson is that our personal experiences and emotional wellbeing can have a significant effect on our professional success, and that cultivating more self-love can help us to navigate these challenges, bring us closer to our goal of being self-made and let us thrive in both our personal and professional lives.

8

Discovering your truth

A guide to self-healing and inner work

I was on a flight home with my two kids after a work trip to Los Angeles in 2017 when I felt a pain in my chest. My breathing was irregular, it felt like an elephant was sitting on my chest and I instantly thought I was having a heart attack.

In an effort not to scare my children, I sat there quietly trying to regulate my breathing and wondering what the hell I should do. I was 35 at the time, healthy (or so I thought), a non-smoker and not overweight. This couldn't be a heart attack, I kept telling myself. The longer it lasted, the more confused I became about what was happening to me.

I couldn't control my short, shallow breathing, and my daughter turned to me and asked me what was wrong. She could sense something wasn't right. I told her I wasn't sure, but everything would be fine. After some time, my breathing began to regulate and the heaviness and tightness in my chest started to subside. Later that week I decided to see my GP about it as it had given me a scare and was not something I had experienced before. I started the conversation with my GP with something along the lines of: 'Recently, on a flight, I felt like I was having a heart attack, however, clearly I wasn't as here I am and I'm fine.' She was kind, and very aware of what had happened to me. She asked me to explain a typical week in my life. I told her I was a mother of two kids who lived with me full-time, I was a small business owner with a team to support, and I was my father's sole carer as he is living with dementia. She told me that she thought what had happened to me on the flight was a panic attack and I was experiencing anxiety. I was shocked and confused. I had been through so much in my life and had never experienced panic attacks or anxiety before, so why now?

I don't know the answer to 'why now?' But, I do know I had too much on my plate, and I was giving so much of myself to everyone else, and not giving anything back to myself. Also, add in the mounting financial pressure from the business, and I was completely depleted. I was giving from an empty cup. This is a common theme that followed me for many years. The doctor explained I needed to make some immediate lifestyle changes and learn to *slow down*. She asked me to start meditating and practicing breathwork daily.

Disclaimer: If you are experiencing anxiety, depression or any other mental health issues, please make sure you seek support or contact a service such as Beyond Blue or Lifeline. While I was asked to practice meditation and breathwork, you may require different treatment. Help and support is available.

As my therapist would say, I'm very all or nothing—zero to a hundred. I started meditating daily and practicing breathwork. I listened to meditation music to calm me down and lit a lot of candles. It seemed to be working. Within a few months my breathing continued to be regular and I hadn't had any more panic attacks. I was fixed! (I realise now, having anxiety never meant I was broken, but I didn't understand that initially. I thought anxiety was a one-off occurrence that I just needed to fix.)

After those first few months, I stopped meditating daily and went straight back to the same frantic pace as before my flight home. I thought I had dealt with the cause of my panic attack and anxiety, and therefore, I didn't need to slow down or change my lifestyle anymore.

Managing your stress and anxiety

While having a type A personality can be an advantage, such as in business and leadership, it can also be a driver that leads to chronic stress, burnout and health problems. It's important for individuals with a type A personality to learn how to manage their stress levels, practice self-care and maintain a healthy work-life balance—none of which I was doing at that time. According to an article on betterup.com,[7] society often associates type A individuals with impatience, extraversion and competitiveness. Type A people add an intense sense of urgency to everything they do.

For me, my desire for high achievement mixed with neglecting my self-care in order to achieve success, and this is ultimately what led to my career burnout in my 20s, and again to my burnout in 2017. Truthfully, I have come close at times while writing this book to experiencing burnout by pushing myself harder than I needed to and expecting too much from myself. The difference is that I learnt from my previous experiences of career burnout, and focused on my self-care. It made a positive difference to both my mental and physical health.

I have now made permanent changes to my lifestyle, because during the global pandemic, my anxiety was at an all-time high. Some weeks I was having panic attacks almost daily, and there were a number of trips to the emergency room for what I believed was possibly a heart attack, even though, deep down, I knew it was most likely a severe panic attack. But as the feeling was so intense, and it was something I couldn't stop, going to the emergency room was what I needed to do to safely come through the other side of the panic attack. At each visit, the doctors would perform the same routine: they would take blood samples, do an ECG and a chest x-ray. Each time the tests showed everything was normal and it was most likely anxiety. After getting the results, my breathing would almost instantly self-regulate, and I would go home feeling more settled.

Anxiety and panic attacks are both debilitating and frightening. Even though I can write that I think I knew deep down it wasn't a heart attack, at the peak of the panic, there's no way I could ride through the experience and wait for it to subside. Your mind is a powerful thing, and anxiety and panic attacks are scary and can alter your logical thinking.

I've tried many things over the past few years to manage my anxiety and panic attacks. Some have been helpful, and others have become less helpful over time. Here are some of the tools I carry daily in my imaginary mental health backpack.

Speak to a psychologist

This is my main tool, and for me, it works well. It's a long-term strategy and won't always help in the moment, but can be really useful for ongoing anxiety management. I am committed to normalising therapy, and I encourage any small business owner who is feeling flat, not yourself, down or overwhelmed to consider seeing your GP for a mental health plan and a referral to a psychologist.

Often, when we think something is a business problem, it can actually be a personal challenge too. In order to navigate the often-stressful task of running a business, you may need to work with a psychologist to equip you with the coping skills to manage the stress associated with running a small business.

This is a topic I am incredibly passionate about. Running a small business is tough, isolating and, depending on the financial status of your business, can be incredibly stressful. You don't have to go through these feelings alone, and from my experience, therapy has been one of my greatest tools and has enabled me to live a mentally healthier life.

Breathwork

This is a powerful tool to calm the nervous system during an anxiety moment or a panic attack. This is one I am still working through as my anxiety affects my throat, and focusing on the throat area can make breathing feel worse for me. It is an effective tool for lots of people though. The box breathing method is a quick and easy technique.

Here are the steps for the box breathing method (illustrated in figure 8.1). You can try it now.

- Find a comfortable seated position and take a few deep breaths to relax.
- Inhale deeply through your nose for a count of four, filling your lungs with air and expanding your belly.
- Hold your breath for a count of four.
- Exhale slowly and fully through your mouth for a count of four, releasing all the air from your lungs.
- Hold your breath for a count of four.

Repeat these steps for several minutes, focusing on the sensation of the breath and the rhythm of your counting. The box breathing method can be practiced anytime and anywhere, and can be especially helpful during times of stress or anxiety. By slowing down and deepening your breath, this technique can help you calm your mind and promote a sense of relaxation and centredness.

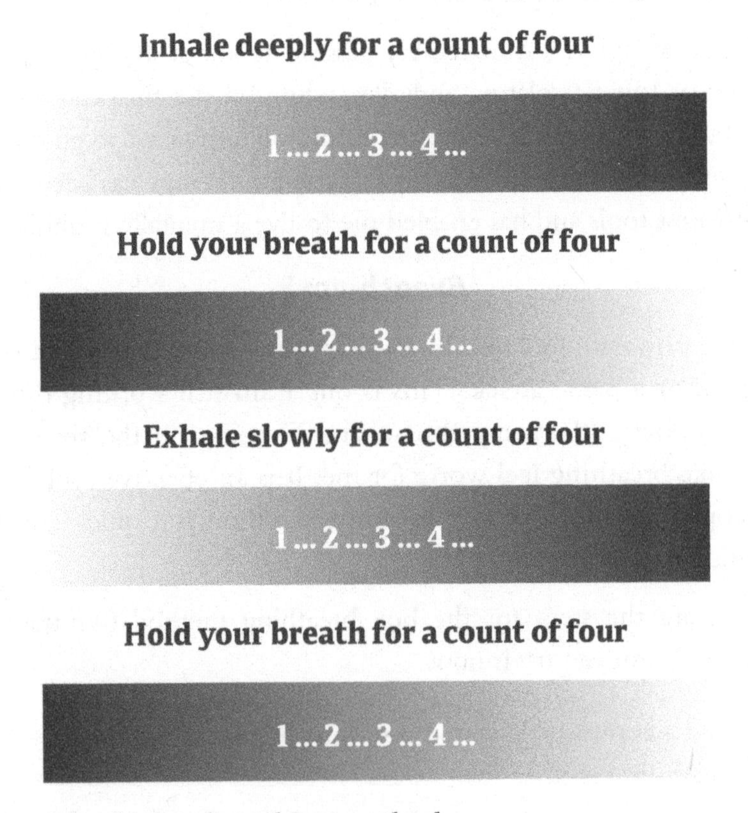

Figure 8.1 the box breathing method

Daily meditation

Breathwork can be helpful when you are in the middle of an anxious moment, but meditation is best practiced regularly, not just when you're not feeling balanced. I love the Calm app and use it nightly before bed. For years I have used guided meditation as I have found this the easiest to commit to. I am now challenging myself to do self-guided silent meditation. The important thing with meditation is not overthinking it or forcing yourself to have a quiet mind. It's honestly just committing to some quiet time every day for yourself.

I also follow Hal Elford's *The Miracle Morning* S.A.V.E.R.S method (silence, affirmations, visualisation, exercise, reading and scribing) most mornings, and have noticed how different I feel. The trick with meditation is to find what works for you, and apply discipline to your daily practice. More on *The Miracle Morning* in Chapter 9.

Exercise

Moving my body a minimum of five days a week either at the gym or on a long walk is an important wellbeing activity. I prefer to do this in the morning, as when I leave it to the end of the day, I feel it's harder to prioritise exercise, especially if you have children.

Holding ice blocks

This one is really effective during a panic attack or heightened anxiety as it refocuses your thinking onto the sensation of the cold object rather than on your irregular breathing. I use this on planes if I am feeling nervous. You just ask the flight attendant for a cup of ice and hold it while flying.

Connecting with nature

I try to walk along the beach or outdoors as often as possible. Connecting to nature is a powerful tool when it comes to stress relief and mental health. There are many studies on the positive effects of nature therapy and mental health and wellbeing.

Audiobooks or podcasts

I always have an audiobook on in the car as it's a great way to get some learning and daily inspiration without having to think about it. Some standout podcasts you might want to try include *The Diary of a CEO* with Steven Bartlett; *On Purpose* with Jay Shetty; *The School of Greatness* with Lewis Howes; *Dear Gabby* with Gabby Bernstein; *EQ Minds* with Chelsea Pottenger; *Little Fish* with Peter Kelly, Dan Reilly and Ben Drohan; and *The Mentor* with Mark Bouris

Solo dates

I regularly take myself on solo dates, such as enjoying a long uninterrupted meal or challenging myself to a creative practice like pottery or painting. The benefit of solo dates is committing to yourself and allowing yourself more moments of pleasure and joy, which are both important for mental health, self-love and filling up your cup.

Journaling

This habit has been a game changer for me. I noticed when I was going through challenging periods that my sleep was one of the first things to suffer. I would take longer to fall asleep, often wake several times during the night and would wake feeling tired. Journaling before bed is a great way to remove the thoughts that may wake you up during the night. It takes less than five minutes most nights, and it has made a significant difference to my sleep.

Follow @drjuliesmith on TikTok or Instagram for more tips for anxiety. Dr Julie Smith is a psychologist and has become famous for her short helpful videos on dealing with mental health.

Consistency is key

Finding the tools that work for you may be a matter of trial and error. Find something that works for you and do it regularly. The mistake I made back in 2017 was stopping my daily wellness and self-care practice the minute I felt better, which was when my anxiety came back ten-fold a few years later. According to everymind.org.au,[8] It is estimated that 45% of Australians may experience mental illness at some point in their lives. Anxiety affects over 2 million Australians each year, which equates to approximately 14% of the population. With statistics like this, we all need to be focusing on our mental health and wellbeing.

Here's the thing I've learned about anxiety, it can come at any time and it may stay with you for the rest of you life. The worst thing you can do if you have anxiety is resist it or try to control it. The best thing to do is learn to manage it.

I believe the body is a powerful machine that is always sending us subtle messages and then not-so-subtle ones if we ignore it. I was ignoring the subtle messages and was not connected with my body at all. I was so focused on building my new business and managing all of the stress that comes with the startup phase that I was ignoring my body all together.

I stopped my daily exercise routine when I started Shhh Silk, and was no longer nourishing my body with nutritional food and energy. I was grabbing whatever food I could get, and eating it as quickly as I could—often skipping meals altogether to keep working. I wasn't getting my daily requirement of sleep, often working until 1 am or 2 am and then starting at 7 am the next morning. I put on 8 kg in the first two years of starting my business, likely from a combination of all of these factors as well as stress.

I was living and breathing the hustle hard, #girlboss culture. I even purchased GRLB0S number plates for my car! Writing this now gives me chills. How did I not see how unhealthy this lifestyle and mentality was, not only for my physical body, but for my mental and spiritual wellbeing. The truth is, at the time, I was honestly proud of how I was operating.

Neglecting your body, your mind and your soul for any period of time is eventually going to catch up with you. My wake-up call was anxiety; for others the diagnosis can be much more severe. I managed to avoid any more panic attacks or anxiety for the rest of 2017 and 2018. I don't know how, as the stress from trying to build Shhh Silk was at its peak during this time.

This lifestyle was no longer working for me. I was feeling so alone, so lost and so unfulfilled and unsatisfied. I had given so much of myself to my business that I could no longer separate myself from it. I felt like I *was* the business. This is not healthy. The harder the business became to grow, the more I felt like I was a failure, like I wasn't capable of creating success, and that I obviously just needed to give more of myself. When would it stop, when would I get to enjoy any of it? When would I get to live my *big*, self-made life. This isn't what self-made success meant to me. I wasn't even drawing a wage from the business. It was sucking all of me: my time, my energy, my passion, my soul.

This is why I started to work with my spiritual coach. I needed to feel connected, I needed to understand I was not my business, and I needed to realign myself to my values and to my true desires.

Doing 'the work', as it's now called, isn't easy. It takes time, patience, commitment, self-compassion, vulnerability and a whole lot of honesty on your part. You need to be open to change, to accept and take ownership and responsibility for the changes you want to bring about in your life.

It's also important to note that there is no end point with inner work. It's a constant journey and one in which you can continue for the rest of your life. I have been on this journey actively now for six years.

So what is inner work?

You've likely heard the term 'doing the work' thrown around a lot on socials. For me, I started with a lot of inner-child work. I'm going to explain what this is from my experience and how I interpret this work. Your inner child is that younger version of you, that free-spirited, loving, curious and connected child. My inner child is around four or five years of age. The age where you still believe anything is possible, and you don't allow restricted thinking to enter your mind. You love yourself deeply and you give love and receive love easily. This is a magical age for me to go back to as it's the time when I remember always wanting to explore and connect with nature. I was still an age where I hadn't developed mentally enough to hold my thinking back. I had a wild imagination, and anything was possible.

I am not a spiritual coach, so I have not gone into the spiritual definition of inner-child work, however, you can research this yourself if it feels aligned for you. Gabrielle Bernstein and Jay Shetty offer a lot of positive content on inner-child healing.

Where the work part of this comes in, is going back to this time of your childhood and remembering things that happened. And memories or experiences that may have left impressions on you and that affect your current beliefs and behaviours. Warning: This can be triggering if you experienced any sort of trauma in your childhood, which most of us have to some degree. I always recommend doing this work with a psychologist to start. In remembering these events or experiences, you can start to work through any trauma you went through and heal the wounds that may still exist because of them. We spoke about money stories in Chapter 2, and often it's through this inner work that you can start to rewrite your money stories, and change the beliefs you have around money based on your upbringing and how money was managed in your childhood.

An example of one of my bigger wounds is that I get anxious easily when my life, my relationships or my business feels uncertain—hence, my anxiety flaring up when the pandemic started. Going through the deep, guided process of inner-child work has allowed me to understand where these wounds have come from and start to work on choosing new beliefs and new stories. I am now able to better manage uncertainty in both business and in life.

This wound has been with me since as long as I can remember. I wasn't aware of childhood wounds on a conscious level until I started doing this work. The hard thing with inner-child work is, just because you now know something, doesn't mean it's easy to change.

Your journey will look different

Deciding to embark on a self-healing journey is life changing, and you will experience deep changes, both personally and professionally. However, it can be incredibly painful at times peeling back the layers of yourself to understand who you are, and why you do the things you do.

My advice is to start small, to find someone that you trust to support you on your journey, someone you feel completely comfortable with. Opening up and doing the work requires you to be comfortable enough to be wide open and vulnerable. You can do this work with a psychologist or with a qualified life or spiritual coach who resonates with you. The reason I have chosen to include this subject in this book is because I don't believe it's possible to become self-made or enjoy true success without doing work on yourself. An example of this is Erin Deering, founder of Triangl, who openly shares on her podcast *The Work* her mental health state when she was at the peak of her $200 million ecommerce business—she was miserable, suffering from mental health issues and feeling disconnected from herself. She couldn't enjoy her financial success as she was seeking more on an internal level. Chasing financial outcomes as the sole measure to living a self-made life is a trap. Becoming self-made and enjoying a meaningful and fulfilling life means you need to have worked on the foundations of what it takes to feel this on an internal level. This is separate to money, material things or status.

Over my six-year self-healing journey, I have seen multiple psychologists, a marriage counsellor, a spiritual coach, a reiki instructor, a kinesiologist, a human design teacher, a psychic medium, a hypnotherapist, a feminine embodiment coach, an intuitive healer and a crystal healing master. There's no one-size-fits-all approach when it comes to self-healing. You need to explore what feels right for you and what feels supportive for your healing journey. It is also okay to see one therapist for a while and then decide to change to another. People come into our life for a reason, season or lifetime. This is the same on your healing journey. You are in control of the journey and you get to choose how the journey looks.

You might be wondering exactly how my self-healing journey has helped me with Shhh Silk. Doing the work allowed me to start to disconnect from my business and reconnect with myself. I learned how to separate myself from my business, reclaim my identity as a human being separate from my business, and balance my ego. The process of separating yourself from your business is really understanding on a deep level that you are *not* your business. You are an extension of your business, but you are not your business. The success or failure of your business does not and should not define you as a person. I started to step back and see myself as an employee of the business, rather than the owner. Importantly, at this time in my journey, I started to draw a wage from the business as well. I would never expect my team to work for free, and you should not expect that of yourself either, especially not a few years in. The added bonus: it was a huge mental win for my self-worth.

Being comfortable on your journey

This decision to go all in on inner work was relatively easy for me, as when you feel burnt out, you are willing to try almost anything to feel empowered and rejuvenated again. I spent several months understanding what had been driving me to work 18-hour days and live the hustle lifestyle. Ultimately, where I landed with this, was that both my ego and comparison were driving this lifestyle. I had been sucked into the vortex of comparing myself to other founders on Instagram who had started their businesses at a similar time to me, and how well they appeared to be running their businesses compared with how well I was doing. This is a dangerous place to be.

Theodore Roosevelt once said, 'comparison is the thief of all joy', meaning that comparing yourself to others will rob you of your satisfaction and happiness. This is also a much bigger problem online, and not just for those running a business. People are comparing their lives, looks, relationships, nutrition, weight, appearance and so on with strangers on the internet. This is your friendly reminder that what we see on social media is usually less than 1 per cent of the person's life and is often fabricated or filtered (or both!). I know this to be true, as in the earlier years of starting Shhh Silk, I portrayed my life as more 'financially successful' than it perhaps was. Now success is extremely subjective; however, when I discuss success in this example, I mean I became unhealthily obsessed with purchasing designer goods, and sharing them online as a metric of success that I felt made me or my business appear more successful to strangers on the internet.

Spoiler alert: This was complete rubbish and was only adding to my feeling of being disconnected from myself and my values. All it was really doing was preventing me from saving a deposit for my first home, or investing the funds into a personal emergency fund: two things that I value more now than pretending to be successful online.

There is nothing wrong with purchasing designer things if you are truly living within your means, however, in my case, my values were out of alignment at that stage in my life. This is also an area I delved into deeply in my coaching: understanding my years of using retail as therapy, only to feel worse shortly after. Retail therapy is a form of distraction or addiction, and something that you can change and get therapy on if you resonate with any of this. I see many women who are running businesses but are struggling to grow them or make them hugely profitable while still purchasing high-ticket items. I never judge them as I have been in that place too; if anything, I want to remind them that you don't need to use labels as a status symbol for success. Don't get me wrong, I love a new Louis Vuitton handbag or a nice pair of shoes from time to time; however, I now purchase these for my own pleasure, not for external validation from others online.

Social media is a highlight reel that only shows the best bits of a person's life or business. Try to remember that next time you find yourself going down the unhealthy rabbit hole of comparison online. This is what was driving me to focus on revenue rather than profit. I felt I needed to reach seven-figure revenue goals with my business in a short period of time to be seen as running a successful business. Once I realised I had been running my business for others and their approval and not for myself, everything changed! The pressure I felt to create something so *big* it was deemed a success was instantly gone. I could actually enjoy my business again. I had perhaps lost sight of why I had started my business in the first place.

Learning that I had been so driven in life by my ego paired nicely with my tendency to compare myself to others. Ego is such a fascinating thing. It is enormously useful and is designed to help us identify our self-esteem and self-worth. Take the title of this book for instance; without a healthy ego, you wouldn't be able to identify yourself as self-made or successful. Like all things, our ego can become unbalanced and need adjusting from time to time. Me sharing my early morning Instagram posts is an example of my ego being unbalanced, and elements of superiority coming through. Same goes with anything we do for external validation rather than for our own joy or pleasure. This has been my life's most expensive lesson, and one that placed enormous financial strain on my previous relationship. We invested far more money than we should have into Shhh Silk in an attempt to build the business faster than it needed to be built—all based on what my ego at the time thought needed to happen.

The reasons I started my business were to have more time with my family, to have the luxury and freedom of being able to pick my son up from school every day, and to be able to give back to the community. It was never about building a business so financially big that I was not able to be a present mother.

To me, *you are already self-made and living a successful life if you can choose how you spend your time.* Making a profit is what will allow you that freedom. It's easy to get lost on the path to success. This is your gentle reminder to course correct your journey, and check in with your ego if you feel like you're currently off track.

If you're thinking about starting a business, please take this one lesson from me. *Build a business that makes you proud first and makes strangers proud second,* not the other way around. A business that makes you money, not one that feeds your ego and leaves you in a financial hole for years. You do not have to have the biggest business to be successful or to live a big life. In fact, the irony is most of the brands I was comparing myself to in the early years were not making much actual profit; sadly, some of them no longer exist.

Another business myth that needs to be busted: just because a business reports revenue in the millions does not mean they are making profit in the millions or profit at all in some cases! This is something I have become very passionate about communicating—helping other female founders understand what they need to do to make money, to have actual cash in the bank, not just make a million dollars or more in yearly revenue.

Most businesses can make a million dollars or more in annual revenue; however, the real art of running a successful business is mastering the art of making profit and managing your cash flow so you have money in your bank account. The following chapters are going to show you what it takes to build a profitable business (the right way).

9

Mastering your mindset

Overcoming obstacles and unleashing your full potential

Henry Ford once said, 'Whether you think you can, or you think you can't—you're right.' To me, this is one of the greatest quotes ever about the importance of mindset. It reminds you that if you believe something is possible, you are far more likely to take action to make it happen or, at the very least, attempt to make it happen. If you don't believe something is possible, you are less likely to try or may give up. You may be thinking: how do you learn to think or believe you can achieve success? Is it something I can learn?

This book has been intentionally written to be equal parts business and equal parts personal development. Not only can you learn to have a growth mindset, but it is critical for success in any area of your life.

I don't know the exact percentage of mindset vs skills it takes to become successful or even if there is one. But I do know from my own personal experience and from the wisdom shared by many sports people, entrepreneurs, actors and so on, that in both business and life, mindset plays a huge role in achieving success.

Reflect back on a time in your life where things felt particularly challenging and you didn't know how you'd ever overcome them, but you did. This may have been a big challenge or a smaller challenge; it could have been leaving a job, losing a job, the end of a relationship, a financial situation or something else. It may have taken you several years to overcome or it may have been a matter of days. It doesn't really matter. Now ask yourself, what steps did you take? Did you enrol in a course or start reading more books or listen to successful people giving interviews on podcasts or Netflix? What helped you get through that time?

Whatever it was that helped you get through that time, chances are it wasn't by staying still and doing nothing. Sure, initially you may have just waited for the moment to pass, but you eventually worked out what you needed to do move through it.

You may not have even realised at the time that it was your mindset or a shift in your mindset that allowed new experiences or opportunities to present themselves so you could get through that challenging period. This is known in psychology as having a growth mindset, and it's crucial for success in business and in life. In this chapter we are going to explore some of the ways in which you can start to develop a growth mindset, which will allow you to experience more resilience, greater motivation, improved learning, more fulfilling relationships, increased creativity and innovation, just to name some of the benefits of having a growth mindset.

So what is a growth mindset?

In Dr Carol S Dweck's book *Mindset: The new psychology of success*,[9] she describes the two ways people view intelligence. If you have a *fixed* mindset, you believe your intelligence is stable, fixed and unchangeable. If you have a *growth* mindset, you believe that your intelligence and your abilities can be improved through effort and learning.

But before we go on, I want to share a real-life example with you of a particularly challenging time for me, a time when I had unconsciously stopped having a growth mindset and the steps I took to get my mindset back into that state.

LIFE LESSON 10: Letting fear take over my growth mindset

During the height of the global pandemic in 2021, I was living in Melbourne, Australia, which was one of the cities locked down for the longest period of time. At some stage during one of the lockdowns, I started to develop some new mental health challenges, particularly around COVID. I was running my business, and trying to keep the team as safe as I possibly could by minimising their close contact with each other, while also trying to balance getting hundreds of daily orders of silk face coverings dispatched as quickly as possible.

I was focused on the daily struggle of living with anxiety and had feelings of constant worry—would my children get ill, would someone I love get sick or worse, and would I ever stop feeling worried about this? The constant noise that I was focusing on around daily case numbers, hospitalisations, and the daily data that was released became an unhealthy obsession of mine. At my lowest point, I stopped feeling like I could safely visit friends and family. I couldn't eat inside a restaurant for fear of catching COVID, and I hadn't been to a supermarket for nearly nine months. Basically, I felt trapped. I wanted to see friends and family and start doing things I loved again. Still, my recurrent worrying thoughts kept me away from doing things I never used to think about.

An endless cycle of thoughts played in my head almost daily for nearly two years, so much so, that I had unknowingly trained myself to start living in fear and worry, and had stopped remembering that I preferred to operate through a growth mindset of positive thoughts of hope, courage, bravery and resilience. When you feel yourself worrying or having 'what if' thoughts, this can be an indicator that you've stopped having a growth mindset, a mindset where challenges and obstacles simply become opportunities for you to grow and develop.

Here are the steps I took to work on developing a growth mindset to overcome this challenging period in my life:

- I opened up to my family and shared how I was *really* feeling, and asked for their support.
- I went to my GP and asked for a mental health plan and decided to start seeing a psychologist.

- I reached out to a psychologist through mymirror.com.au (I chose an online psychologist as it offered me flexibility regarding times). I chose weekly therapy sessions for the first three weeks, and then I moved to every couple of weeks until I was on track with my new positive daily habits.
- I started re-reading self-development books, specifically around courage, hope and new habits. I recommend *Stop Playing Safe* by Dr Margie Warrell, *The Book of Hope* by Jane Goodall and *Atomic Habits* by James Clear. I hadn't discovered the powerful book *The Miracle Morning* by Hal Elrod at this time, but I highly recommend it.
- I wrote myself a list of all the goals I wanted to achieve in the next 30 days. I ranked them from least uncomfortable to most uncomfortable based on where I was at. I started with the least uncomfortable, and worked up to my most uncomfortable, which was flying internationally again. That goal took me another year to accomplish, but I felt so empowered when I achieved it. (Examples of some of these goals were: eating outside at a restaurant, getting my hair done, going inside a supermarket, going to a shopping centre, seeing a movie, flying, staying at a hotel, and so on.)
- I committed to walking in nature daily. Numerous studies have found that nature reduces your stress.
- I returned to my favourite wellness and healing centre in Melbourne, and re-commenced kinesiology sessions.
- I started journaling to release my anxious thoughts and better understand what I was worried about. And I started writing things down that I looked forward to, things I was grateful for and things that I had already achieved.

- I used positive self-talk to replace any unhelpful thoughts I was having when I felt worried. I would bring myself back to the present moment and remind myself that in that moment all was well and I was safe.
- I focused on small consistent efforts rather than just the outcome. Rather than aiming to fly internationally straight away, I started taking actions to place myself in environments that were indoors and gradually more and more confined, until I was finally ready to take a short-haul flight, and then a longer one and then a solo flight, and then worked towards my first international trip.

For me, it was never about the fear of contracting COVID. It was much deeper than that. COVID was simply just another life event which I felt I had no control over. I felt 'out of control', which triggered my anxiety and worry mindset.

I continue to do the daily work of replacing my unhelpful thoughts with better ones. I am constantly choosing again. If I have a thought about how hard it is to make our targets due to the economy, I stop myself in the thought and I choose again. I train myself daily to be a solution seeker.

Important to mention

I want to acknowledge in this life lesson that I have referred to mental health, which is a complex health condition and not something that can be treated fully without seeking help. I have included a list of services at the end of this book you can reach out to for support or help if you or someone you know is struggling with mental health.

One of the most common questions I get asked on my social media from female founders is how to see a therapist. You are not alone if you are feeling like you need to speak to someone. I am aware that mental illness can be such a varied illness, and the treatment is rarely the same for any two people. I am sharing my personal story not as a way to offer medical advice, but to help others realise they are not alone. I urge you to seek help if you are struggling, feel stuck or simply haven't felt aligned in yourself since COVID or any other traumatic event you may have experienced.

The role of positive thinking

When it comes to starting, growing and running a business, I know it takes a positive growth mindset to be able to succeed. Business has many ups and downs, and working on your mindset parallel to growing your business will make the journey feel more manageable, less overwhelming and more enjoyable.

As the founder of Shhh Silk and Self-Made Academy, I have the privilege of speaking with ecommerce founders daily, and the other frequently asked question I receive is, 'Did you ever want to just give up?' Truthfully, I think most, if not all, founders will tell you that they thought about giving up almost daily in the early years. And even as recently as the beginning of 2023, I wondered if running my own business was really worth it (thanks to increasing interest rate rises and a reported slump in retail spend). This is where feelings of fear try to creep back in again, with unhelpful thoughts of 'what if'. Instead, I switched my thinking to a more helpful thought of *'what can I do?'* in this market to grow and succeed?

I first discovered the power of positive thinking and personal development in my early 20s. I was working full-time as a real estate agent and had met my first mentor, Andrew, who I talked about in Chapter 2. He had self-taught himself to have a growth mindset, think positively and have an abundance mindset. I was fascinated by his confidence, achievements and mind. He had achieved so much material success at such a young age. All these years later, I can still recall so much detail about my experiences being mentored by Andrew. The way he was always well groomed, the fact that his clothes were always freshly pressed and dry cleaned, he wore nice cologne and cufflinks, he was always clean shaven, and his car and home were immaculate. He owned lots of books and CDs on self-development and had taken many self-development courses. He would later go on to run one of Australia's largest self-development organisations, where I would later become a sales manager.

Andrew has been the most impactful mentor I have had in my life so far. It's often the people we meet along our journey to becoming self-made that have the most significant impacts on our mindset. When you meet someone, whether it's your boss, a fellow founder or business mentor who is already living the life that you desire, you can start to model behaviours or habits they display. They become your teachers for success. You can learn so much from the people you choose to spend your time with.

You have all likely heard the saying, 'you're the average of the five people you spend the most time with', a quote attributed most often to motivational speaker Jim Rohn. Well, this is absolutely true. If you spend most of your time with five millionaires, you're likely to become the sixth. If you spend most of your time with five negative Nancy's, you're likely to become the sixth. Who you spend most of your time with has a significant impact on your success and on your mindset. It can be a really challenging exercise to make a decision to be more conscious of who you spend your time with.

ACTIVITY

Your circle of influence

Grab your notebook and pen and write down the answers to the following questions.

- Who do you have in your circle of influence currently that is living the life that you desire: a self-made life? (Remember, success for each of us means different things.)
- If you can't think of anyone in your current circle, imagine someone famous. Who is it?
- What is it about their life that you want to emulate?
- What daily habits do they have?
- What are all of the intricate details about this person that you can study, and that you can learn from?
- What steps will you take to introduce these habits into your daily routine?
- Who are the five people you are currently spending the most time with?
- Do these people have a growth mindset?
- Do these people display the lifestyle you want?
- Who do you need to start spending more time with?

- What actions can you take to spend time with these people?
- Who do you need to start spending less time with?

If you couldn't think of someone within your circle who is living the life that you desire, where can you find someone? There are many places to surround yourself with positive, like-minded individuals in business. Places like networking events; connecting with people via their online accounts on LinkedIn, Instagram; industry groups; or even Self-MadeAcademy.com.au.

Why is having a growth mindset so important for success?

As I mentioned earlier, your business journey (and life journey) will be full of unexpected challenges, obstacles and setbacks. Without doing the daily work to build your positive mindset muscle through activities, such as reading self-development books like this one, it can be easy to have a fixed mindset reaction or feel triggered when you are faced with a challenge or setback. This could be a voice within your head that says this is too hard, too much or you simply start to feel overly anxious. This is what happened to me in the life lesson example I shared, and it took me over 12 months to choose to think and act differently and take the steps to retrain my growth mindset again.

In business, having a positive mindset will allow you to get curious and creative during challenging periods, such as economic downturns or slower retail months. Rather than giving in to the notion that you can't do anything to change the situation, and remaining defeated and static, you will be able to explore multiple ways to get through the challenging period and come out the other side stronger.

Adversity reveals character, and the harder the challenge, the more you need to dig deep, get creative and resourceful, try multiple things until something works and then you repeat this process over and over until you have overcome the hurdle you were faced with.

Have you heard the saying, 'If it were easy everyone would do it'? This is also true when it comes to running your own business. On some level you knew starting your own business was going to be tough at times. You may have underestimated just how tough starting and growing a business was going to be, but with the right mindset, you can learn to succeed.

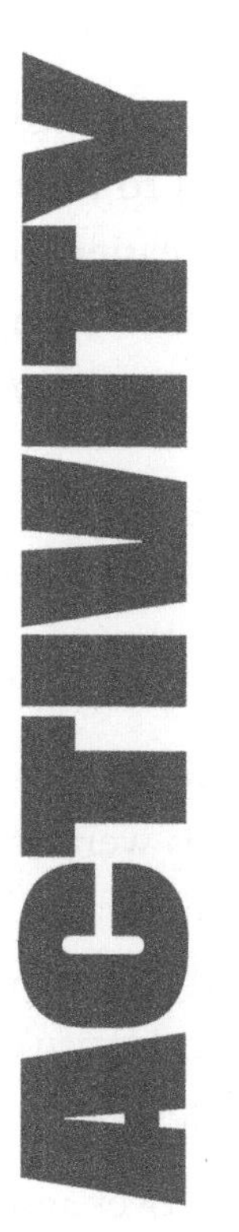

Applying a growth mindset to your business

Grab your notebook and pen again as it's time for some honest reflection. Take your time to really think about each question, as the more detailed your responses, the greater results you can achieve. These questions will allow you to see where you can do some work on your mindset within your business to achieve greater success:

- What things currently feel too hard within your business or in your life?
- What is causing them to feel hard?
- Can you think of some solutions for these things?

- What are the steps you can put in place to take daily action to make them feel easier or more achievable?
- Who or what can you do to seek guidance from or support for these things?
- Are you putting in as much effort as you really could to try to succeed in these areas?
- Do you find yourself procrastinating on achieving these things?

Write yourself a goal for each thing and what you are going to commit to doing this year to achieve success.

I know, myself, in the past when things started to feel a little hard or the results weren't where I thought they'd be, I started to look externally for reasons or excuses as to why. It was often easier to blame external factors such as the economy or a pandemic than to roll your sleeves up and do the daily work required to continue to see results within your business.

Time to go inwards

After doing years of self-healing work, I developed more self-awareness, and I started to see that, usually, the reason things weren't where I wanted them to be, was me. I had become less motivated, I was procrastinating, I had stopped doing the small daily actions I needed to take each and every day to grow my business. I wasn't being proactive, creative, determined or trying new things.

The definition of insanity is doing the same thing over and over and expecting a different result. When things are no longer working within your business, you need to ask yourself, what can I do differently, what else can I try today to achieve success? And, importantly, ask yourself, why am I not doing the work that it takes to make this business a success? Be really honest with yourself. It's okay to have moments of rest. If you feel less motivated than usual and you're procrastinating, it may be to avoid having to get uncomfortable and apply the level of self-discipline you know deep down is required to achieve and sustain success. You can acknowledge that; I still have moments like that. What I do now is take a break. I have learnt that I need to fill up my cup regularly. You cannot pour from an empty cup. It is within that level of self-awareness and honesty that you can discover something new about your current mindset that you can work on to achieve more resilience, greater motivation, improved learning, increased creativity and innovation, and greater success.

At this point, I want to say that in no way am I suggesting you grind, hustle or burn yourself out by doing whatever it takes to succeed. Far from it. I do not subscribe to the hustle culture that exists within business. (Been there, done that, we all know how that ends.) What I am suggesting you do is get honest with yourself about areas for growth within yourself.

This may mean you need to take time away from your business to fill your cup up and work on your mental wellbeing. Often what I do is take a mini two-night escape, book a session with my therapist, go to the gym and head to the beach for a long walk. But, importantly, I remove myself from the office and don't judge myself for feeling that way. I realise I cannot be *on* 24/7 and I need to rest and recover. It's crucial that you allow these moments of recharge to help you re-energise to get back to the daily discipline it takes to achieve success within your business.

You may be reading this and realise you haven't taken a trip away in years as you've busy working on your business and that is exactly what you need, or you may realise you haven't been investing the time daily into your mindset, and you resonate with some of the earlier examples. Your external world is a reflection of your internal world. If you want to achieve more success and earn more freedom for yourself, it is time to do more of the internal work.

I recently updated my morning routine with suggestions from *The Miracle Morning* by Hal Elrod. However, you can adapt your routine to suit your lifestyle. The most important step is creating time and space first thing in the morning to focus on your self-development before the day slips away from you. Here are some ways in which you can create a success-focused morning routine.

- Wake up at the same time every day (even on weekends). Give yourself at least one hour before you need to start getting ready for work or getting your children ready for the day. This is your solo time.
- Start with a short meditation, either guided or silent. If you are going to use guided meditation, there are thousands on YouTube or you can download an app such as Calm. You can also try affirmation videos by typing in 'I AM affirmation meditations' in YouTube and choosing one of the I AM meditations. 'I am' are two of the most powerful words when it comes to affirmations.
- Introduce some slow stretching like yoga or deep breathing into your morning routine. You could also choose to do any form of exercise that increases your heart rate, gets your blood flowing and wakes your body up.
- This next one is powerful: visualisation. Create a vision board either digitally using Pinterest or Canva, or a physical vision board and make time to review this board with intention each morning. Your vision board should include goals that you are working towards to create a self-made life.

- Use this book or another self-development book as part of your morning routine. Choose a section that resonates with your intention for the day.
- Journal. This can be reflections, things you are grateful for, or even your intentions for the day.

You can add more things into your morning routine, such as an outside walking meditation, combining both meditation and exercise. You could even try taking a cold shower. The point is your morning routine should be customised to what feels nurturing and supportive to you. And should have a focus on activities that support your mind and self-development.

Some of the benefits I have experienced from having a consistent morning routine are more energy (ironic, as I've never woken up as early as I do now), more sustained focus at work, more focus on tasks that are aligned to my goals, and less procrastination. I feel as though I am vibrating at a different frequency. I feel more motivated, and I am radiating energy. I was able to write this book with far more clarity each morning.

Win the morning, win the day

Grab your notebook and make a commitment to yourself about what you are going to introduce into your morning routine from tomorrow. No excuses. Each time we make excuses for our own self-development, we are not allowing ourselves to get closer to success or to grow as a person. I understand we each have our own daily routines and some people will have small children to get ready, others will work night shifts etc. Whatever time you usually wake up, make a commitment to yourself that you will wake up earlier each day to work on yourself. I wake up one hour earlier than I normally do, and I no longer need an alarm. If that feels too much, start with 10 minutes earlier, and once you've experienced the benefits and the mental shifts, you will see the value in dedicating more time for yourself each day. My advice would be to include as many of the activities I mentioned in your daily routine. But, most importantly, start your day with time just for you, before you start giving from your cup to others.

A morning routine is another great example of how a growth mindset encourages us to focus on effort and process, rather than simply outcomes. If you put regular, consistent effort into your morning process, success will follow. But if we wake up each morning and attach our thoughts to achieving a certain number of sales that day, without doing any work on our internal mindset, the chances for the success will be inconsistent and perhaps non-existent in more challenging retail environments.

Your external world is a reflection of your internal world, so the more effort and process you put into your internal self-development, the more success you will experience in your external world.

Tips to remember when it comes to self-development

Consistency is the most important step of the process. The time you dedicate each day is not as important as the consistency of a self-development process or routine.

There will be times where things happen, and you may let your routine slip. Be compassionate with yourself, speak kindly to yourself and just make a commitment to re-commence your routine today.

Different things work for different people. I love to read daily, and use meditation in my morning routine. You may find a daily yoga practice and affirmations and visualisation is your preferred self-development.

Get curious. If you don't usually use visualisation, give it a go. Commit to 30 days and see how it feels. If you can't commit to yourself each day, it's going to be near impossible to commit to growing your business each day. The more discipline you can practice, the more results you will achieve.

Be kind to yourself, be patient, trust in the process. You've got this. When your mindset and positive thinking starts to shift, I promise you, your external world will start to shift also.

10

Unlocking the secret to success

Taking action

In 2020, I started my mentoring business for women who have their own ecommerce brands or want to start one. My love language is acts of service, and I receive so much joy from my monthly sessions with these women. But after several months, I noticed a pattern.

Almost all of the women were experiencing similar challenges in their businesses. They felt that their businesses weren't quite where they needed them to be financially to take the next step, which was often hiring their first team member or moving out of their home office.

We would go through their business financials and monthly numbers, and create an action plan to move them from point A to point B. We would agree on what they would focus on for the coming month, and they would leave the session feeling empowered, re-energised and less overwhelmed.

The idea of the action plan was to break down their bigger monthly goals into bite-sized daily steps to move them towards achieving their desired outcome.

As we discussed in Chapter 9, it's more important to focus on the process than it is to focus on the outcome. If you don't take daily action or follow a disciplined process, the outcome is simply a desired dream. A goal without a plan is just a wish, likewise, a goal without action is also just a wish. As Pablo Picasso once said, 'Action is the foundational key to all success.'

These women would return the following month and we would always start the session by reviewing the actions they had committed to for the month.

Nine times out of ten, their agreed actions were not complete or even started. There were always excuses as to why they hadn't been able to action them, and so it would go. We would have a discussion about this, and we would reset some actions for the following month.

After a few months or so of this pattern, I started to become more and more curious as to why these women, who all had businesses with the potential to succeed, were not committed to taking the action necessary to grow.

Sure, they were taking some action, and would have bursts of discipline, but there were more periods of no action. I soon realised that each of these women had their own stories and belief systems about why they weren't doing what they knew was required to grow.

Self-limiting beliefs

A lot of these stories (self-limiting beliefs) were a result of their own mindsets and lack of belief in themselves to achieve success. An example of a limiting belief I heard a lot from these women is, *I am not good at sales.* What these women needed to work on was changing their beliefs around their ability to make sales, and stop focusing on the outcome. To start doing the internal work and get to the bottom of what limiting beliefs they were carrying that were blocking them from taking the action required to achieve their desired outcome (which I believed they were all capable of achieving). This level of self-work takes time, patience, self-compassion and kindness. And it takes a lot of honest self-reflection. We all have beliefs from our childhood or past experiences that are potentially holding us back, so it's important to work on your belief systems in order to live the life you want to live.

I covered a lot of the ways you can start to focus on your mindset in Chapter 9, however, in this chapter, I want to explore ways in which you can start some of the self-healing work that is necessary for you to feel inspired, confident and motivated to take the daily action that is required for success within your business and in your life.

So grab your notebook and pen and let's do some self-discovery work.

Reframe your self-limiting beliefs

- What is one belief you feel is currently holding you back from taking the necessary steps to achieve greater success in your business?
- Is this belief accurate?
- Where do you think this limiting belief comes from?
- How can you reframe or rewrite your limiting belief in a positive way? (For example, I am not good at sales can be rewritten as I have the potential to become great at sales, and I am committed to learning and improving my skills to achieve success in sales.)
- Write down the steps you can take right now to start overcoming this limiting belief.

Repeat this process for any other limiting beliefs you may be experiencing.

The transformative power of self-belief

When it comes to your self-limiting beliefs, it's important for you to be able to first recognise and acknowledge the blocks you may be experiencing mentally that are preventing you from experiencing the level of success you desire.

It is when we become stuck, and we can't see our own blocks, that acknowledging these can be more challenging. To help get clarity on this, you need to go through an internal process of radical self-acceptance of where you are now, identify where you want to be and decide on the steps you need to take to bridge the gap.

Radical self-acceptance is the opposite of avoiding responsibility or giving up in self-defeat. It's about pushing against old ways of being, knowing they are what opens the door to healing at the deepest level. In doing so, we give ourselves the opportunity to integrate our shadow aspects and live more authentically.[10]

It is only once you have gone through this process of realising and accepting your current limiting self-beliefs that you can begin to do the mindset work to reframe and retrain those thoughts. This is a process I go through from time to time when I have my own limiting self-beliefs, like being able to finish writing this book!

Another term that has become popular in business circles is 'imposter syndrome'. While imposter syndrome is similar to self-doubt, it is important to understand the difference between feeling like you are a fraud and experiencing feelings of self-doubt. Let's unpack what imposter syndrome is.

What is imposter syndrome?

If you've ever felt that you don't deserve your success, that everything you have is due to luck or being in the right place at the right moment, then you may be experiencing imposter syndrome. If you've ever felt that people see you as more intelligent, business-minded, or creative than you feel—and you worry they are going to suddenly realise that you've been faking it all this time—that could be imposter syndrome. That constant niggling feeling that you'll one day be exposed as a fake (or an imposter) can trigger feelings of anxiety and fear.[11]

LIFE LESSON 11
When imposter syndrome and self-doubt creep in

In 2016, Shhh Silk started experiencing incredible media moments featuring our products in the hands of some of the world's biggest celebrities. I was interviewed by some of the most prominent media outlets about the growth and early success of Shhh Silk. This type of exposure early on in my business journey meant that I started to build a brand presence for Shhh Silk that, at the time, I felt gave the impression that Shhh Silk was bigger than it was revenue-wise.

I felt that people would soon discover that Shhh Silk was not this gigantic overnight success that the celebrity moments were making it appear to be. To this day, Shhh Silk is still primarily known as the brand that blew up after Kim shared our products on her apps and website. While I am, and will always be, beyond grateful and incredibly blessed to have experienced these genuine, unsponsored celebrity moments with the likes of Miley, Selena, Khloé, Kim, Kylie, and so on, the truth is, at that time Shhh Silk was struggling financially, and I was beginning to fall apart.

When I look back at that period of my business journey, I placed so much emphasis on revenue and monetary success that I couldn't truly celebrate the moments for what they were—phenomenal! Instead, I felt like a fraud. How could I possibly let anyone know that, despite these incredible celebrity moments, I hadn't quite learnt how to operate my business financially, and I wasn't even drawing a wage?

Over the years, the feeling of imposter syndrome passed as I learnt that, regardless of the financial status of my business, all of the incredible celebrity moments were very real. They were all a result of my relationships and networking.

If you are feeling like a fraud, it's very likely that this feeling extends only to you and no one else. It could also be a sign you are living out of alignment with your values (we cover more on this in Chapter 13). Remember, this is your life; you don't owe anyone an explanation for how you choose to live it.

What I learnt from this

I now handle all media interviews and questions with transparency. I no longer need to share inflated future financial goals or aspirations for the business. These are irrelevant and just make good clickbait ('Teen mum to $50 million silk sleepwear empire', or similar). In the past, when self-doubt or imposter syndrome crept in, it became easy to mask my reality with fabricated versions of what was really going on for me and my business. Being honest with where the business was at during the pandemic, particularly financially, was immensely empowering. I was able to overcome my feelings of imposter syndrome by focusing on how grateful I was when a celebrity shared our brand, and reminding people what a privilege it is to have that sort of support as a small, family-owned business.

I also reminded myself that people weren't judging Shhh Silk on these moments; they were genuinely excited that the moments happened. And for many people, it was those insane moments that made Shhh Silk so unique and so successful. The other stuff was all just in my head.

As I've shared with you in this book, my personal measure of success is more than the financial results of Shhh Silk, or the number of likes or mentions we receive on social media. I still have enough self-doubt to prompt me to do the inner work on myself, and like most people, I still experience some self-limiting beliefs; however, on the other side there is always growth, and that's my highest value.

This is exactly the same with launching or growing your business. *The only thing stopping you, is you.*

Moving forward with your business

There is no real *secret* to becoming self-made or successful, however, if there was one defining trait that would give you the best chance of success, in my opinion and experience, that trait would be *action*. Daily, regular, consistent action. When I started the process of getting myself out of debt, I took small daily actions towards climbing out of that situation. You can use this same strategy to help you move forward from any current circumstance you find yourself in. Set small daily steps to move you towards a new life for yourself.

Let's look at how you can achieve more success in your life by taking action now.

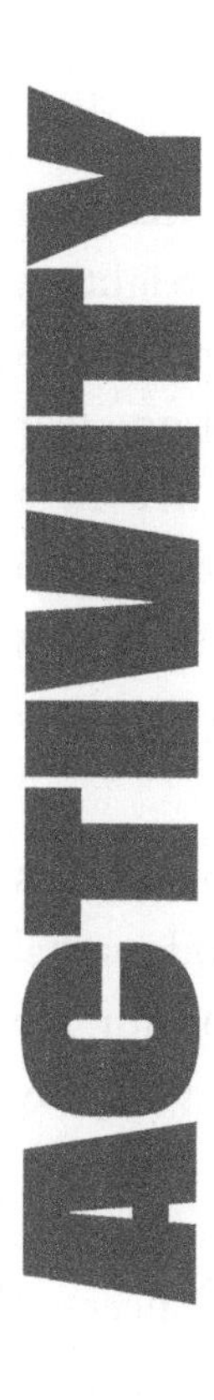

Taking steps to move forward

Write down the actions you are going to take using the following questions.

- What tasks have you been putting off?
- What actions can you commit to taking immediately to achieve them?
- If you need help or support with these tasks, who or where will you go for help?
- Can you break these tasks down even further into individual steps to make the outcome easier to achieve and less overwhelming?
- What are some new daily actions you are committed to taking in the next few days to help you achieve more success in your business?

Aside from your own limiting beliefs, there are some other things that can make it difficult for people to take action.

The reason taking action is so important to success is because you can't become successful by not taking action. The key is consistent action to build momentum. The more you do something, the easier it becomes.

Working through fears

The Oxford dictionary describes fear as: 'the bad feeling that you have when you are in danger or when a particular thing frightens you'. Fear is a complex emotion that we all experience and that is often not real. During the early stages of human evolution, fear was designed to protect us from danger, however, we live in a different time now. While fear can still be useful in helping us to avoid dangerous situations, it can also cause us to avoid situations or activities, interfere with our experiences and prevent us from reaching our full potential.

Fear is an emotion I am very familiar with. I was more fearless before experiencing anxiety in 2017 than I am now. Fear and mental health is a complex issue for many people to navigate, and for me that has meant working through my fear-based feelings with my psychologist on a semi-regular basis. I shared in Chapter 9 how fear stopped me living my life the way I wanted to live it during the pandemic. To continue to run my business and achieve the success I desired, I needed to work through these fears to be able to take action.

It seemed impossible for me to take daily action to work towards being able to fly to America in 2021 for work. I had developed a new fear of flying, which was linked to my anxiety at the time. When I really started to work on this fear, and do the inner reflection work, I was able to recognise that I was actually afraid of something going wrong or, deeper still, surrendering complete control while in-flight (which we all do each time we fly, it's just most of us do this subconsciously).

I don't share this example lightly, as I know fear of flying is a real phobia for millions of people and it can be debilitating. I'm sharing it because I was able to do some really important and meaningful inner mindset work with my psychologist around these fear-based thoughts, and I am now back to flying internationally again. Are the fear-based thoughts completely gone? No, but they are more manageable.

Understanding what's within your control

Feeling out of control, or that I have no control in my life, causes me to feel very uneasy and, at times, anxious. One of the greatest concepts my psychologist has taught me is the circle of influence, made popular by the author Stephen Covey in his book *The 7 Habits of Highly Effective People*. We all have three circles (as shown in figure 10.1). The large outer circle is known as the circle of concern, the middle circle is the circle of influence, and the inner circle is the circle of control.

The largest circle, the *circle of concern*, represents the things that we worry about, but may not have any control or influence over, such as global events, natural disasters, dying, or other people's behaviours.

The middle circle, the *circle of influence*, represents the things that we have some influence over, but may not have direct control over, such as our relationships, environment and other external factors.

The small inner circle, the *circle of control*, represents the things that we have direct control over, such as our thoughts, behaviours and actions.

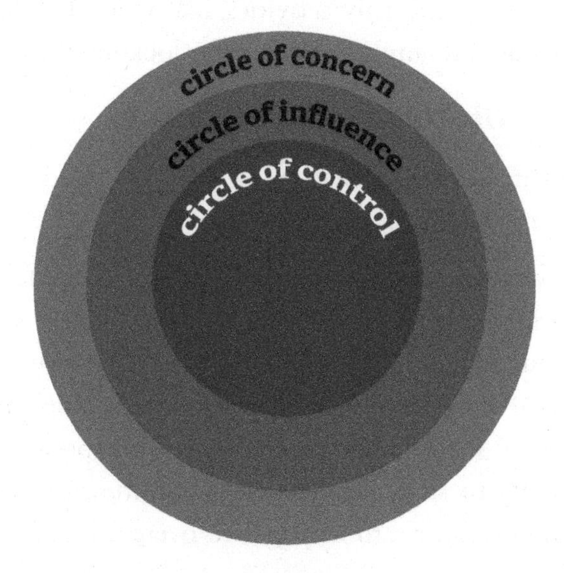

Figure 10.1 the circle of influence

Adapted from 'The circle of influence' taken from Stephen R. Covey's book, *The 7 Habits of Highly Effective People*

It's no surprise that during the time I was experiencing heightened anxiety, I was focused on the large outer circle most of the time. I was worrying about all of the things that were out of my control, such as the global pandemic, and people I loved getting sick and perhaps even dying.

Once my therapist shared this concept with me, something in my brain clicked. It resonated so strongly with me that a couple of days after learning about this concept, I took my first flight.

I was able to do that by focusing on the small inner circle every day, controlling my thoughts, behaviours and actions. I was still a bit nervous during the flight, but I kept bringing my thoughts back to what was in my control. I observed the behaviour of the cabin crew (a highly effective strategy for anyone with a flying phobia) and could see they were calm and happy, which influenced how I was feeling.

It is only when you identify and work through your fears that you can start taking action. It's also important to seek help from a professional if you feel like your fears are starting to take over your ability to do your normal daily activities, like when I stopped being able to visit friends and family well after the lockdown had ended.

Obstacles and roadblocks

These are real-life situations that get in your way and prevent you from taking immediate action.

A practical example of this in business is wanting to launch a website but having no idea where to start. Or wanting to start wholesaling your products but having no idea what price to offer your product to stockists.You have most likely already come across multiple roadblocks on your journey to success. Start to see them as temporary stop signs, but not an excuse to stop. They are opportunities for you to seek solutions and find resources to help you to overcome these obstacles.

One of the easiest ways to do this is to use your network for advice. It is highly likely that what you are faced with now, others have encountered, and have worked their way through. Or you can find useful resources online to help. You can read books, listen to podcasts or even seek a mentor in the field you are working in. Join a community of like-minded individuals (like my online community Self-MadeAcademy.com.au) and use the support of that network to help you move past the obstacle.

Another great proactive exercise you can do is create a list of possible obstacles you may encounter on your business journey, along with possible solutions so that you've already prepared for them. This is an important step in effective goal setting, which we will cover in Chapter 13.

So grab your notebook and pen and let's try to break down some of your current obstacles and roadblocks now.

ACTIVITY

Breaking down roadblocks

Think of a goal and list all of the practical obstacles delaying you from moving forward and taking action.

List a possible solution for each one, including who you can ask for help or where you can go for a solution.

Are any of your obstacles related to lack of finances? If so, write down some possible solutions and actions for working through this. For example, can you access additional revenue from other revenue streams, such as wholesale or marketplaces?

If you can't find solutions for an obstacle, ask yourself if you have any self-limiting beliefs or fears around not thinking you can achieve this?

If you identify particular self-limiting beliefs that are holding you back, revisit the Reframe your self-limiting beliefs activity on page 146. Remember, the more you open your mind, the more opportunity presents itself.

If you noticed most of your obstacles were related to your mindset or limiting beliefs, you may find it valuable to seek some support from a psychologist or a business or life coach. Speak to your GP about a mental health plan, which has the added bonus of qualifying you for financial subsidies for therapy. I have listed more about this at the end of the book.

Dealing with internal roadblocks

Sometimes the roadblocks you face will be less practical. You might struggle with a lack of accountability, discipline or commitment to yourself. You might find distractions in your physical environment.

Making sure your workspace is clutter free, inspiring and, ideally, not in your bedroom is really important. Try to disassociate your workspace from your bedroom, as that is where you go to rest and recover.

Sometimes you'll face challenges that are more about dealing with the attitudes and opinions of others. If you feel like you don't have a voice at the table as a woman in a leadership role, I've listed some strategies that you can apply to make sure your ideas and contributions are valued and respected. It's also important if you are managing a team, or you have employees, that you are supporting women to have equal opportunities in the workplace.

Here are some actions you can take to stand up for yourself, and for other women, in your role:

Speak up

You should never be afraid to speak up and share your ideas, opinions and perspectives. It is important to assert yourself in meetings and discussions, and make sure your voice is heard.

Build allies

You can build relationships and allies with your male and female colleagues who support and amplify your voice. Allies can help you navigate workplace politics, advocate for your ideas and provide you with emotional support when you need it.

Develop expertise

You need to develop expertise and knowledge in your field, which will give you more credibility and influence. This can be done through training, professional development and by staying up-to-date with the latest trends and research. Never stop learning your craft.

Negotiate

You should negotiate for yourself and your ideas, whether it is for a promotion, a raise or more resources for your team. Negotiation skills take time and can be learned. They can help you achieve your goals and gain more influence in your workplace.

Challenge bias and discrimination

Challenge bias and discrimination when you encounter it, whether it is through reporting harassment, speaking out against stereotypes, or advocating for more inclusive policies and practices. Someone in the retail industry who is a powerhouse for women is Kate Morris, Founder of Adore Beauty, who is a vocal advocate for gender equality in the workplace.

The most important thing to remember about breaking the glass ceiling is that it's about creating equal opportunities for everyone, regardless of their gender or other personal characteristics. Breaking the glass ceiling means overcoming the barriers and challenges that prevent women and other under-represented groups from advancing in their careers and reaching their full potential.

Breaking the glass ceiling is not just about promoting individual women to leadership positions, it's also about changing the systems and structures that perpetuate gender inequality and discrimination. This requires addressing issues such as bias and stereotypes, unequal access to resources and opportunities, and the lack of representation and diversity in leadership positions.

Breaking the glass ceiling is an ongoing process that requires the collective efforts of individuals, large and small organisations, and society. It is important to continue advocating for gender equality, supporting and mentoring women in the workplace, and creating inclusive and equitable work environments that allow everyone to succeed and thrive.

As a small business owner, you have an incredible opportunity to be part of these efforts in your own organisation. What a truly special privilege that is. Use that privilege wisely. Even if you are a sole trader, you have the opportunity to make an impact on important matters.

Take action

Now that we have covered some of the things that may be blocking you, it's time to create a plan to take small, consistent, daily actions towards your desired goals.

Grab your notebook and pen again and let's get started.

ACTIVITY

Get started!

Write down the most important task you want to start working on right now.

Break this task down into as many small, individual tasks as you can. (The more small steps you have, the easier they will be to achieve.)

Next to each individual step, write 'by when', and insert the date you will complete this task.

Next to each individual step, write 'how long', and insert how long you think the task will take in total to complete. If it's more than a couple of hours, you may need to break it down further into smaller steps.

Now, decide how many hours or minutes you want to dedicate to these tasks each week, and create an action plan to achieve the tasks.

Transfer these tasks to your daily to-do list or calendar.

On the following page I've provided a fairly simple example of a task to find a local packaging supplier for your ecofriendly ecommerce mailing satchels.

Task: Finding new ecofriendly mailing satchels

Task	By when	How long	Complete?
Google search for ecofriendly mailing satchel suppliers in Australia	Sunday 19th March	30 minutes	YES
Fill out online enquiry form for three of my preferred suppliers for costs and samples	Tuesday 21st March	15 minutes	YES
Place an order online with my preferred supplier	Tuesday 28th March	15 minutes	YES

Some of the tasks on your list will have many individual steps. The most important aspect of achieving consistent action is to make sure you only allocate yourself the volume of tasks that you are able to dedicate time to per day or week. If you only have three hours a week to work on your business idea or on your task list, then make sure you only allocate three hours' worth of tasks.

Remember to choose the *right* tasks, not the *easy* ones. Prioritise the ones that are going to help you achieve success sooner. If you have a business, you should always be focusing the majority of your time and effort on revenue-generating tasks, not just tasks that you find easy or enjoyable. If you find you struggle to achieve some of the more urgent tasks as they are uncomfortable or challenging, you may like to read *Eat That Frog* by Brian Tracy.

11

Sustainable growth

Build your business from your values not your ego

It took me just over four years to realise I had wasted so much money trying to build Shhh Silk into a big business overnight. Throwing money at every opportunity that came my way, from trade shows in America, to gifting thousands of products in the first few years to PR events, spending over $100 000 on a business coach ... the list goes on.

You do need to be willing to try a lot of different things when you are building your business, however, not at the expense of making a profit year after year as a self-funded founder. This is where my ego really did get in the way of how I was operating Shhh Silk in the early years. It is not easy to admit it publicly, but it is the absolute truth. It is so easy to get caught up in comparison—something I have touched on throughout this book.

We're going to revisit this topic again, as I know it is something you will face (or have faced) with your business. It can be one of the biggest reasons why small businesses overspend on the wrong things and don't make profit sooner. The feeling that, unless your brand makes more than $1 000 000 in revenue you haven't really succeeded, comes from a place of your ego. And once you hit your first $1 000 000 year, you need to get to the next milestone, and so on and on it goes.

Your business revenue is *not* the most important metric for your business. When you are self-funded, the most important metrics you should be obsessing over are your profit sheet and your balance sheet (i.e. how much actual money you have in the bank). The irony is, some brands that make less than $1 000 000 in revenue are definitely making more profit than brands that are making more than $1 000 000 in revenue. Don't ever forget that. I was caught up in this almost instantly with Shhh Silk, having launched at a time when it seemed like most of the brands on Instagram were killing it.

No one I knew in 2015 was talking about how much profit they were making. It was all about how many followers they had gained, how fast their revenue was growing and who was using their product. None of this is wrong, but when you are a self-funded founder who isn't making profit, and you're comparing where your brand is against where you think your competitors or other brands in the industry are, it can make running a business from a place of ego rather than values easy to do. You start making decisions for your business based on what everyone else is doing and not what feels aligned to you, your business or your financial capacity.

In a year where revenue *and* profit for Shhh Silk were down, instead of trying to keep up and compete with others in our space, I dropped back into a *values mindset* by asking myself what the business needed at that time. We focused on introducing *lean* practices and right sizing the operation for the headwinds. If you are curious how you can improve the efficiency in your business, I suggest reading *The Lean Startup* by Eric Ries.

Since the beginning of 2020, I have become known in the retail industry as a founder who will openly share my numbers and the profitability of Shhh Silk in an attempt to make other founders feel less alone. I aim to make talking about profit rather than revenue more normalised. This level of openness only changed for me after I spent time getting back to being aligned to my values and why I started Shhh Silk in the first place.

You can build and run your business from a place of alignment with your values, which will ultimately focus you on building a sustainable, profit-making business that is meaningful and makes an impact.

Let's look at what it means to build a business from ego versus values.

ACTIVITY

Ego vs values

Tick any of the boxes below that currently apply to you.

- ☐ Comparison: A founder who is focused on building a business from their ego may be overly concerned with what their competitors are doing, constantly comparing their business to others, and making decisions based on what they think will make them *look* better than their competition, rather than *what is best for their own business*.
- ☐ Status: A founder who is building their ecommerce business from a place of ego may prioritise status symbols, such as having a fancy office, expensive equipment or luxurious perks, over making sound business decisions that will help the company succeed.

- ☐ Overspending: A founder who is driven by their ego may spend money frivolously, such as on flashy marketing campaigns or expensive business trips, without considering the impact on the company's bottom line.

- ☐ Lack of focus on profitability: A founder who is building an ecommerce business from a place of ego may be more concerned with how their business appears to others, rather than focusing on generating profit. This could lead to a lack of attention or focus on important metrics, such as customer acquisition costs or ROI, and income versus expenses, which will ultimately harm the company's financial health.

If you ticked any of these boxes, you are not alone. Prior to 2020, I ticked all of them, several times over! Ironically, while I was operating the business from a place of ego, Shhh Silk did not make profit. This exercise can be hard to accept, but it may open your eyes to some changes you need to make, both internally and for the profitability of your business.

See this exercise as a blessing, as it's through understanding and true acceptance of what is driving the poor performance of your business that you can turn things around—just as I did. And the good news is, it can happen a lot faster than you may realise. By running your business from a values-based mindset, you will not only see tangible financial benefits, you will start to feel more aligned and successful.

LIFE LESSON 12
Sustainability and efficiency over ego drives better business outcomes

Over time, my values as the founder of Shhh Silk became more embedded into the business I was building, and our product offering, packaging and branding started to evolve.

When Shhh Silk launched, I (my ego-self) aspired to be in every beauty brick-and-mortar retailer regardless of the demand, because I believed that achieving this is what would make us a successful brand. This would grow our top and bottom line, which is very important in business, but there are so many other factors to consider in addition to numbers when it comes to building a good business. Tip: It also requires a large injection of capital investment to expand your brand into retail distribution, margins are small and you need to be able to fund the orders. There are financing options for this, but this is also something that is not discussed openly. Retailer margins can be incredibly tight, and for your brand to achieve success it's a scale game. You need to scale your brand.

More so than scaling, being a thoughtful, considered and sustainable brand became hugely important to me. It felt very aligned to my values and the original purpose of Shhh Silk. Don't get me wrong, being able to grow and scale your business should 100 per cent be a focus. I am constantly working on ways and ideas to continue to scale Shhh Silk, however it's through a more sustainable lens. I reached out to Story Folk, a small female-founded branding agency in Melbourne, to collaborate with them on rebranding Shhh Silk to align with our values and purpose. During this year-long partnership, we were able to not only rebrand our visual identity and solidify our brand messaging, but also work towards being a plastic-free packaging brand. This is something I am hugely proud of. And, yes, while it's considerably more expensive to use recycled and recyclable paper for your packaging, for bigger and more important reasons, single-use plastic should not be an option for your brand.

As well as moving to becoming a more sustainable brand through our product development and packaging, over time, my values have allowed me to strategically take a step back and really look inside myself and consider whether my business is still aligned and on the same path as my values. It's so easy to get pulled in different directions and lose sight of your initial intentions of starting your brand. I encourage you to regularly check in with yourself.

A more recent example of this playing out for me, was my decision not to actively keep pursuing large beauty brick-and-mortar retailers that already stock the market-leading brand in our space. This is probably fascinating for you to read this, so let me share with you why I landed at this decision. When I sat deeply with myself in April 2023 and asked myself if pursuing these retailers aligned with our brand's core value of doing good, my answer was 'no'. It was a no, not from the point of view that I didn't want Shhh Silk to be stocked on the shelves of these high-profile stores; that would be incredible for the brand and our customers. It was a no from the point of view of true sustainability.

Our product's core ingredient is 22 Momme, high-grade 6A mulberry silk, which is the identical core ingredient as the market-leading brand. So, for the consumer, the only real difference comes down to price or the core brand values. So, I now feel that approaching beauty retailers that already stock a silk pillowcase doesn't feel aligned sustainably. Placing another product with the identical ingredient side by side, even with more sustainable packaging and a different price point, is just product excess and not sustainable or necessary for such a niche product category.

For Shhh Silk to be aligned with its core values of doing good, we need to live by that statement and not mass produce for the sake of mass producing. Instead, we find products our customers currently don't have access to in physical spaces and direct them to our website.

We are not a mass-production brand. We are, and always have been, a small sustainable, family-run business that creates meaningful impact and prides itself on doing good. This decision didn't come lightly, as I was working with a retail distribution specialist to align our brand with beauty retailers. We agreed to stop pursuing retailers that already stocked the market-leading brand. I realise in sharing this, this may be music to their ears, but I choose to share it more so to challenge other founders not to chase opportunities purely based on revenue and growth alone.

Do the work

As a founder, sometimes you also need to respect that there will be other brands bigger than you, that perhaps existed before you, with larger capital and resources than you have right now, and that have already done the hard work in building out certain markets. You can't expect to just land in the same space as them without doing the same work, making the same investments to build those opportunities.

I am in no way saying you shouldn't pursue these opportunities; I am reminding you that you are going to need to invest the same work and capital that other brands have to land those opportunities. And it may not be time for your brand right now. You need to be patient and realistic about where you are right now, what is possible for your brand right now and work towards achieving these opportunities when your brand is in a position to do so.

Some of these deals with large retailers will require a huge amount of capital and logistical capability, so it's important you are prepared for that. And it's important to ask yourself if your business cash flow is ready for this type of deal and if you have the capital to support the deal (or where you will get the capital from). There are many lenders you can use to access funds for large deals like this, so if you feel ready, you do absolutely have options. Take risks with retail growth; just make sure they are calculated. Shhh Silk took a risk on a very large deal in 2017, and we didn't end up getting paid for close to 12 months. That caused a ton of additional stress and put massive financial strain on the business—it was also one of the factors that contributed to my mental burnout in 2017.

This is where building a values-based business is important as, depending on your product margins, you may not always make a profit when working with large retailers. Silk pillowcases are an expensive product to produce, and the margins aren't as flexible as other beauty and cosmetic products. So when beauty retailers charge a retail margin of 50 to 70 per cent, you need to make sure this works for your brand.

In the early years, I would have signed one of these large deals regardless of the financial outcome, just to have Shhh Silk seen in the big stores. Not anymore. Always work with someone who can do your financial modelling when you are looking to enter into large agreements with brick-and-mortar partners (stores). There are a lot of costs involved, and you need to make sure it makes sense for your brand. This is a great example of how running a business from your values over ego looks in real life.

I trust that opportunities that align to our core mission of doing good will present themselves. I trust and believe we will organically continue to find our white space in the larger ecosystem, without having to mass produce products, and make meaningful impact. To any retailers reading this, if you currently have white space in your physical stores for a sustainable and meaningful brand that exists to do good, then I am very excited to connect and have a conversation.

Follow your own path

Choosing to grow your brand slowly, ethically and sustainably will also make it easier for you not to get caught up in the comparison trap of focusing on where your competitors are stocked, who is using their product or how many stockists or retail doors they have. It's not healthy for you to focus on this. I know it sounds easy for me to say this, but I promise you I share this lesson from a space of love and genuine care for your success and your mental health. I have been down this road and it's a dead end and a waste of mental space and energy. It will also just steer you off your own path. If you are always comparing your success or current traction in the market to other brands that have been in the space for longer, you are going to do more damage than good to your mindset and self-esteem. Focus on what is really important to you and the mission and impact you are setting out to achieve with your brand, and have faith that you are where you are meant to be. Stay focused on values and impact. It's a kinder space to be.

I acknowledge, having been there, how easy it is to fall into the ego trap when you start to build your brand.

Consider your impact

You may think that you need to be in every store or shop window across the globe, but the truth is, the world needs less now, not more. As a founder in the ecommerce space, you have a responsibility for the part that you and your brand play in the environmental impact of entering the consumer space.

This isn't a book on climate change, but I do want you to take that responsibility seriously when you are building your brand. What impact does your brand have on the environment? How can you make your footprint on this earth as light as possible while still building a sustainable and profitable brand? It can be easy to get swept up in all of the products you see ads for on Facebook selling the current gimmick or the hottest trend that will disappear as fast as it came. Absolutely, you can make some quick cash from starting a business off the back of this model, but this is not what building a long-term, sustainable and meaningful brand is.

If you have been considering selling or dropshipping products that are hot and trending now, instead of designing a sustainable, long-lasting brand, ask yourself how this model aligns with your core values. Does the idea of moving a lot of product that will likely end up in landfill in a matter of months make you feel inspired and proud? I'm guessing the answer is 'no'. If you are dropshipping or selling the latest

Facebook product, how can you take your desire to build and scale a trending product and turn it into a hugely successful, more sustainable and profitable brand? This is something that should make you feel inspired and proud. Be the brand that others turn to for inspiration.

I am no longer a lover of creating products for the sake of creating products. We all need to do better with overproduction and overconsumption of consumer goods. Choose more sustainable products and be more responsible when developing your new product or business idea. This is why Shhh Silk launched its made-to-order sleepwear service in 2019, and it's why all of our products are made with environmentally friendly natural fibres, like silk, bamboo and cotton. We use our offcuts for silk hair scrunchies and always look to innovate with products that our consumers actually want. You can build a hugely profitable business by selling products that are gentler to the planet.

If I were to build a new product-based business today, I would start with a sustainability focus that prioritises quality.

The truth is, I now believe, what makes you a good brand is being conscious, considered, not adding to landfill or overproduction, and doing good—whatever that looks like for you and your brand. Just being aware and committed to doing better is a huge part of being a values-based brand.

ACTIVITY

Defining your brand values

Tick any of the boxes below that currently apply to you.

- ☐ Authenticity: Does your brand truly reflect your values, beliefs and vision?
- ☐ Customer focus: Are the needs of your customer at the forefront of every decision?
- ☐ Purpose-driven: Do you desire to have a positive impact on the world? Are you guided by a strong sense of purpose?
- ☐ Sustainability: Are you conscious of your brand's impact on the environment and society? Have you taken steps to reduce your carbon footprint, source products responsibly or support social causes?
- ☐ Efficiency: Are you operating a lean business that reduces waste, minimises overhead costs, and maximises profitability without compromising on its values.
- ☐ Long-term success: Are you approaching your business relationships with a long-term focus that will create a loyal customer base that will continue to support you, even during tough times.

How many of the boxes applied to your business today? Are you able to spot the opportunities where you can move your current business to being a more aligned, values-based business? If you are a founder who is already operating a values-based business, you should absolutely be so proud of yourself—you are on the right path, stay there!

12

From solo to team

Navigating the challenges and opportunities of when to grow your team

One of the hardest decisions to make in your business is knowing when to hire your first team member. It can be incredibly challenging and scary. Knowing when to make this decision and when the right time is can be hard. So I want to help guide you through this decision based on my experience, as having someone else's livelihood to consider, as well as now being responsible for their professional development and growth, is a serious step for your business. And on top of that, you will have extra pressure on your business cash flow.

I get asked by a lot of small business ecommerce founders who I mentor when they should hire their first team member and what role it should be. This answer is different for everyone; however, my feedback on the first question is: *not until you absolutely have to*. When you are first building your business, you need to be as efficient as possible with your time and resources. As Henry Ford once said, 'If everyone is moving forward together, then success takes care of itself.'

LIFE LESSON 13
Shhh Silk's first hire

After running Shhh Silk from my spare room for the first 19 months, I decided it was time to hire my first team member, and get a serviced office in Melbourne. The business was ready for its first hire: a core function that I had no skillset in, and would help our growth. At the time, I felt it was unprofessional to have someone work for me from my home study.

Who did I choose for my first hire, and why? Being an ecommerce brand means a lot of content creation is required for marketing and brand awareness. In order for me to grow Shhh Silk and work on new partnerships, I knew I would need support with that. In the first year and a half, I used Canva to create as much content as I could; however, as the brand started to grow, and the technical requirements for product development increased, so did the need for a graphic designer. To make sure I was making a sound decision with my first hire, I reached out to a trusted colleague and asked her who her first hire was. (Being able to ask others in the industry what they did and how they did it is invaluable.) She shared that it was a graphic designer.

Having a graphic designer in-house would allow me to oversee the design and lead the direction of the work created. I hired a final-year graphic design university student three days a week. The first task she worked on was designing the patterns that I would present to The Beverly Hills Hotel (more on this in Chapter 14).

From a cash flow perspective, I wasn't paying myself a wage at this point, and it was tough paying a team member and a lease and storage fees when we were not yet making a profit. During this time, personal funds were still being poured into the business to keep it alive. This was the beginning of a very financially stressful and challenging time. Somewhere along the way, I lost sight of what was essential, and decided to grow the business and the team, and move into an even bigger office space (another ego-self decision). However, I was making a big mistake. I was growing the business overheads just as fast as our revenue was growing. We were still not making a profit! This is not how you build a lean operation and not how I would ever mentor a brand to build and grow its business today. I was so swept up in the belief that bigger meant better, and that's just not the case at all. Truthfully, looking back over that period, the business could have been managed with just one graphic designer and one person to dispatch orders and myself running sales, marketing and operations.

But I learned a valuable lesson about balancing resources in my business. Today, we have a team of seven, and aside from me, none of the team is full-time. I have a lead graphic designer three days a week, an operations and accounts lead three days a week, and four casual warehouse staff.

Out of the team of seven, four of us are family. Working with family could be a chapter on its own! The first four or five years of being my mother's boss was challenging. I had to seek a lot of guidance on how to switch between daughter and boss, and the same went for managing my children. If you are hiring family, I strongly urge you to seek guidance or coaching on the dynamics and complexities a family business faces. You can also reach out to organisations like familybusiness.org.au for courses and resources to help guide you through the process. It's also important to remember when you have family and non-family employees that the dynamics can be challenging.

Looking to the future of Shhh Silk, our current plan is that the lead graphic designer will transition to a freelance model, our operations lead (my daughter) will leave the business when she starts her career in accounting, and we will be back to five people in-house.

Leading your team

One of the greatest joys of building a brand is growing a team and creating your own unique business culture. Before starting Shhh Silk, I had managed teams in organisations I worked for; however, leading a team within my own business did not come naturally to me for some years (and I still find it challenging at times).

As your business grows, it becomes increasingly important for you to learn to lead more than do. I am a natural 'doer' and doing comes very easy to me. I am fast paced and being an effective leader requires skills that don't always align with that—mainly patience. I am working on this. If, like me, you employ family, you will also need to learn healthy boundary setting and effective communication.

Overall, it is truly special to be able to nurture, mentor and develop your employees, and to prepare them for their next role (or their own business). You should also not underestimate the time and energy commitment required to foster and build a highly effective team.

Some business owners shy away from hiring older members of the workforce—I have a team ranging from 16 years old to 69 years old. The value that mature-aged workers can add to your small business is invaluable.

It's also important to be open about the kind of work culture you want and live those values daily. We have an incredibly flexible, close family-feel culture at Shhh Silk where we foster a culture of continual growth and openness. For us, an applicant's potential culture fit and energy can be just as important as their skill set.

As your business grows, so will your team, and it's really important to make the right hiring decisions and ensure you have a culture that you want to work in every day and are inspired by. I am hugely grateful to every employee who has been part of the Shhh Silk journey and helped us to continue to grow and evolve. Even the staff who have left Shhh Silk to travel the world, gain new skills or start their own businesses have all taught me things about myself.

Right sizing your business

There's no magic formula of how many staff you should have, or the exact percentage your payroll cost to revenue should be (it varies by industry, but generally for retail, it's around 20 to 30 per cent). People costs typically include salaries, benefits, payroll taxes, superannuation, and other expenses associated with employees, contractors or freelancers.

So if you are generating $1 000 000 in revenue, you don't want to be paying more than $200 000 in total people costs (ideally). You need to take into account your situation as, depending on your profitability, $200 000 could still be too high.

In the third year of Shhh Silk's operation, Shhh Silk was spending 22 per cent of its total revenue on people costs. In theory this is in line with the retail industry (bear in mind I wasn't earning a salary at this time), but the business made a *loss* that year. So based on the actual financial position of the business, a lower spend on people costs was one consideration I should have made. In Shhh Silk's most profitable operating year, our total people costs were 16 per cent of our total revenue and I was paying myself a salary. And Shhh Silk made a net profit of 19 per cent. That is how I should have been running the business from the beginning.

My hope is that by sharing these lessons with you, you don't have to make the same (avoidable) mistakes I did. I am at peace with my business journey, as I am now able to use my experience and knowledge to empower and mentor other women to grow their businesses the right way. Just as I am doing now.

If your ecommerce business is not yet making a profit, it's important that you approach your people costs cautiously, as they can quickly become a major expense that eats into your business' financial resources.

Since the beginning of 2020 when the pandemic touched Australian shores, and I nearly had to close Shhh Silk, I have been far more focused on efficiency and running a *lean*, profitable business than a business that has a high expense-to-revenue ratio.

Do you have to hire someone?

A valid question to ask yourself is whether a traditional employee model is right for your business. Thanks to a greater ease in and acceptance of remote working, you have so much more flexibility about how you choose to grow your team these days. A good intermediate step is to work with a qualified freelancer or agency, though you may have to persist and try a few vendors until you find someone who gets your brand and your vision. When I started Shhh Silk, there were not as many agencies that handled content creation, but this is something you have lots of access to today, so outsource what you can before hiring in-house.

When you're ready to grow your team, be excited, be financially and legally prepared, and also tread carefully in the beginning. As your profitability grows or shrinks, scale your team accordingly.

Grab your notebook and let's explore whether you are ready for your first hire.

Your first hire

Are you constantly overwhelmed by your workload? If you find that you are regularly working long hours and are unable to keep up with the demands of your business, it may be time to consider hiring your first employee or outsourcing some of these tasks. Answer these questions to help you narrow down some of the logistics around it.

- What tasks do you feel you need help with? Do you have the skillset to perform these tasks?
- Do these tasks require an in-house person or can you outsource them to a freelancer?

- If you need someone in-house, do you have a clear job description and list of responsibilities for your new hire? Before hiring your first employee, it's important to have a clear understanding of what you need them to do and what skills and experience they should bring to the job. Think about how they will be measured based on performance.
- Can you afford to pay a competitive salary and benefits? Hiring an employee comes with significant costs, including salaries, benefits and payroll taxes. Make sure you have a clear understanding of the costs associated with hiring your first employee and ensure your business can afford this.
- Are you ready to be a manager? Hiring an employee means that you will need to manage and delegate tasks, provide feedback and guidance, and potentially deal with any employee issues that arise. Make sure you are prepared to take on this role before hiring your first employee. Managing a team member will take time out of your day. You need to be ready to offer your time to your employee to help them grow and succeed.
- Will your new hire bring a valuable skillset or fresh perspective to your business? Hiring your first employee is an opportunity to bring in new skills and perspectives that can help your business grow and succeed. Make sure you are hiring someone who can bring something valuable to the table.
- Do you have the legal employment contracts and employee handbooks that your employee needs? If not, reach out to a service such as Employsure to make sure you are legally ready to employ someone, as you may also need to consider things like workplace health and safety and Workcover. There are changes to your business when you hire someone.

13

Measuring success

Revisiting your purpose, values and goals to track progress

When I first experienced career burnout just four years into running my first business Shows 4 Kids, part of the problem was I had forgotten to revisit my purpose, values and goals. Purpose is such a heavy-hitting word and people often approach it with a lot of apprehension, curiosity or confusion. So many of us wonder 'What is my purpose?' or 'How can I find my purpose?'

I don't have the answers to those two questions for you. However, I do have some thoughts and ideas on how you can find the answers for yourself. I also believe our purpose and values are not static and can evolve as we continue to grow and develop.

The power of purpose

When I think back to my younger self, my purpose behind wanting to become a famous actress was to be able to connect with and entertain people through my performances. When I started Shows 4 Kids in my 20s, my purpose was to entertain and educate children on some really important lessons, such as cyber bullying and healthy eating and exercise. This aligned with my values at the time; however, I don't think I was passionate about this purpose. It didn't drive me or fuel fire within me to do whatever it takes to live out this purpose. I wasn't aware at the time of any of this, of course; I was in my mid-20s and had not done any personal development work to understand my purpose and my values.

When I started Shhh Silk, I was 34 and had experienced some significant personal development and life experience. I knew the importance of having a strong *why* or purpose behind my brand. That purpose remains strong and ingrained in my brand today. The purpose behind Shhh Silk is to do good and make a positive contribution to the community. Doing good is in our DNA. The brand itself started with my promise to my eight-year-old son that I would build a brand that would help others.

It's this *why* behind my brand that fuels my passion and provides me with the dogged determination to keep going, even though it feels like the odds are stacked against me. The difference between why I have kept going with Shhh Silk (despite also experiencing burnout in 2017) and why I walked away from Shows 4 Kids is purpose.

My business purpose aligns with my personal purpose, which is to be able to make a meaningful impact through regular acts of kindness and giving. That might mean giving financial support, donations, time, effort, energy, advice, mentoring, support, inspiration or even an act as simple as a smile to a stranger.

When you find your purpose and it aligns to your business, rather than feeling as though everything is too hard, you will be more likely to look for ways to find solutions, as you want to be able to fulfil your purpose.

Grab your notebook and pen and let's see if we can work out what your current purpose is.

ACTIVITY

What is your purpose?

Think about these questions as you reflect back on your life experiences.

- Can you think of a time where you saw, heard or experienced something and you had to stop and take action?
- When you are your happiest, or lightest, what are you doing?
- What things make you feel really good?
- What moments in life stand out to you?
- When you catch up with friends, what do you find yourself always going back to in conversation? What lights you up when you talk about it?
- If money were not a consideration and you didn't have to think about it, what would you be doing?

- What things do you like watching on YouTube or social media that fill you up?
- What does living a *big*, self-made life look like to you? Describe it in as much detail as you can.

Now these are big questions, and you may not be able to answer them straight away. But the seeds have now been planted, so next time you find yourself talking to friends and smiling and feeling really passionate about something, stop and make a mental note of it. This could be the start of understanding what your purpose is. I think it's also important to understand that your purpose doesn't need to be life altering or grandiose. It's most important that no matter what your purpose is, it aligns to your values, interests and passions. It should feel meaningful to you, and that's ultimately what I believe to be the most important thing when getting clarity on your purpose.

If you have previously gotten stuck trying to work out your purpose, you may have been thinking too big. I encourage you to come back to your simple pleasures in life: things that light you up, things that make you feel like you have direction and meaning, and that you are interested and passionate about. You don't need to search externally for your purpose, it already exists within you. You just need to be able to identify it by working through some of the questions or examples in the activity. And, remember, purpose isn't static so it can change over time.

Values guide your journey

Values are an important part of what makes you who you are. They are what gives your life meaning and they influence the decisions you make in life, business and relationships. Values can also be developed and strengthened through self-development.

You may desire to live your life with certain values, however, you may need to do some self-discovery work on how to live that value. An example for me is my desire to live life with the value of self-respect, which will help me to live my life with more self-love and self-worth. However, there have been circumstances in my life that have impacted my self-respect and self-worth and meant I don't always live my life upholding the value of self-respect.

In order to be able to develop and strengthen my desired value of self-respect, I need to continue doing the self-healing and development work to get to the root cause of my lack of self-worth. Examples of this can include things like setting healthy boundaries for myself, not people pleasing, learning to say 'no', speaking kindly to myself and having compassion for myself. So, while I may desire to have the value of self-respect, I need to do the work to be able to live my life from a place of self-respect, and this takes time, practice, acceptance and development.

When we look at the values list on the following page, you may be in the same situation. There may be values you desire to display and live by, but there are things preventing you from living by them fully right now. That is a normal part of growth. So we are going to look at your current and your desired values.

ACTIVITY

What values do you live by?

Grab your highlighter and highlight your *current* top five values, in no particular order. If you can't find a value in the list, insert your own.

Accountability
Achievement
Adaptability
Adventure
Altruism
Ambition
Authenticity
Balance
Beauty
Being the best
Belonging
Career
Caring
Collaboration
Commitment
Community
Compassion
Competence
Confidence
Connection
Contentment
Contribution
Cooperation
Courage
Creativity
Curiosity
Dignity
Diversity
Efficiency
Environment
Equality
Ethics
Excellence
Fairness
Faith
Family
Financial stability
Forgiveness
Freedom
Friendship
Fun
Future generations
Generosity
Giving back
Grace
Gratitude
Growth
Harmony

Health
Home
Honesty
Hope
Humility
Humour
Inclusion
Independence
Initiative
Integrity
Intuition
Job security
Joy
Justice
Kindness
Knowledge
Leadership
Learning
Legacy
Leisure
Love
Loyalty
Making a difference
Nature
Openness
Optimism
Order
Parenting
Patience
Patriotism
Peace
Perseverance
Personal fulfilment
Power
Pride
Recognition
Reliability
Resourcefulness
Respect
Responsibility
Risk-taking
Safety
Security
Self-discipline
Self-expression
Self-respect
Serenity
Service
Simplicity
Spirituality
Sportsmanship
Stewardship
Success
Teamwork
Thrift
Time
Tradition
Travel
Trust
Truth
Understanding
Uniqueness
Usefulness
Vision
Vulnerability
Wealth
Wellbeing
Wholeheartedness
Wisdom
Write your own:

Now Brené Brown suggests that you narrow this list down to your two core values.[12] This is incredibly hard if you're like me and find a lot of this list important to you. I suggest you choose the five that are currently non-negotiables, and then out of those five, choose the top two that feel most aligned to you.

Your values will help you identify and live out your purpose in alignment. Right now for me, my top two values are growth and giving back. They still align deeply with my purpose of being able to make a meaningful impact. When you feel you have identified your top two values, you may experience even more clarity around your purpose. And you also may not, which is fine too.

Looking at that list, you may also find you have values that you *aspire* to live by, and this is really useful too. We are going to do another exercise now to capture some of the values that you are curious about. This can be a great way to continue to grow and develop.

ACTIVITY

Exploring your values

Let's explore your values a little further. I have included space for you to write them in this book, as you may like to revisit them from time to time.

List your top two current values below or in your notebook.

____

____

Write down what each of these values means to you and why they are important.

____

____

____

___

___

Are you living these two values in your life and your business? If yes, how? If no, what is holding you back?

___

Is there anything you could change in your business to expand on these values?

___

___

___

List the values that you would like to explore further.

1. ___
2. ___
3. ___
4. ___
5. ___

What is it about these values that is important to you?

___

___

___

___

Finally, what are some steps you can take to introduce these values into your life and business? What do you need to start doing, keep doing and stop doing?

____

____

____

____

____

____

____

____

____

S.M.A.R.T. goals

Before I get into goals, let's look at what goals are and why they are important. Goals are intentions you set for yourself that can provide you with direction and motivation and provide a measurement for success or progress. It wasn't until I worked for one of Australia's leading personal development companies that I truly developed an understanding of what a goal is and how to structure a goal. The concept of a S.M.A.R.T. goal (illustrated in figure 13.1) was developed by George Doran, Arthur Miller and James Cunningham in their 1981 article, 'There's a S.M.A.R.T. way to write management goals and objectives'.[13]

Figure 13.1 the S.M.A.R.T. way to set goals

How I was taught about S.M.A.R.T. goal setting was to write your goals in the following structure:

SPECIFIC: Really get into the detail. Write down the who, the what and the why.

MEASURABLE: How will you know when you achieve your goal? What tools can help you track this (metrics, clicks, sales)?

ATTAINABLE: What do you need to achieve your goal (money, staff, time)?

REALISTIC: Have you set the benchmark too high? Too low? Can you achieve what you have set out to do?

TIMELY: Give yourself a deadline. Work back from that deadline to ensure it's realistic and attainable.

LIFE LESSON 14: Resetting Shhh Silk's business goals

When I walked away from my first business, Shows 4 Kids, another important lesson I learnt was the importance of reviewing and resetting your goals. Just as our purpose and values can change or develop, so too can our goals. My initial goal for Shows 4 Kids was a monetary milestone. What can happen with business goals if you reach them but don't reset them is that you can start to lose drive and motivation to continue to grow your business. Or, in my case, when I didn't stop to reset my goals, I reached the four-year mark, felt burnt out, lacked a sense of purpose and I walked away. Now, I don't have many regrets in life, but I wish I knew the importance of resetting my business goals. This includes reviewing your purpose, looking at your current values and then aligning your goals to your purpose and your values.

With Shhh Silk, even though I had a strong sense of purpose for the brand from its inception, I wasn't always able to fulfil that purpose in the way I would have liked from the beginning due to the lack of profitability of the business and having the wrong goals in place. When I experienced my second burnout, I remembered the lessons from walking away from my first business. Instead of walking away, I chose to re-evaluate my business goals and align them more closely with my purpose and values. For me that included lowering my initial revenue growth goal and reframing to having impact goals. This meant focusing more on growing a profitable business that would allow me to make an impact as opposed to continuing to try to scale my business and return low (or in some cases no) profit, resulting in a smaller opportunity for impact.

This felt counterintuitive to me, initially, as one of my other values at the time was being the best I could be. And by pulling back on or reframing my revenue goals for the business, I felt as though I was falling short of my potential. The truth is, if I had continued striving for aggressive growth with everything else I had on my plate, like raising my children as a single parent, being my father's sole carer and managing the team, I would have continued to feel burnt out and that mental state is not a healthy place.

So going through the process of asking myself what I valued most allowed me to understand that I wanted to feel less stressed, less anxious and live a more balanced, self-made lifestyle. So instead of walking away, I started to do the work to develop some new values, such as freedom, financial stability and balance. This was the turning point for me, and also the moment that I slowly started to unsubscribe from the hustle, grind and #girlboss culture that can exist within the entrepreneurial space.

I started to value the freedom to do more things for myself that made me feel more balanced, successful and worthy. These changes were my personal definition of living a *big*, self-made life. A life where I get to choose where and how I spend my time, how and what I invest my personal wealth in, and how I get to give back and make a meaningful impact. The interesting part about this is that my value for drive and success never changed, they just took on a new meaning. Once I had established a new roadmap for myself, I was then able to reset some of my business objectives and goals and start to experience and live my self-made life.

Irrespective of where you are at in your business journey, let's take a deep dive into your past, current and future goals. Grab your notebook and pen.

ACTIVITY

Resetting your goals

Write down your answers to the following questions. If you are just starting your business, skip to the current goals section.

Past goals

- When you first started your business, what were your goals?
- Why were these goals important to you?
- Are they still important to you?
- Do they align with your current purpose and values?
- Do they inspire you?
- Do they drive you to want to accomplish them?
- Are they meaningful to you?

Current goals

- What are your current business goals?
- Why are these goals important to you?

- Are they still important to you?
- Do they align with your current purpose and values?
- Do they inspire you?
- Do they drive you to want to accomplish them?
- Are they meaningful to you?
- Are they in the S.M.A.R.T. format? If not, write them down using the S.M.A.R.T. goal-setting structure.

If you answered 'no' to any of these questions, let's reset and reframe some of your current goals.

Reframing your goals

Use your answers to the past and current questions to identify any gaps or changes you want to make. Write down some new goals for your business.

- Why are these goals important to you?
- Do they align with your current purpose and values?
- Do they inspire you?
- Do they drive you to want to accomplish them?
- Are they meaningful to you?
- What needs to change for you to work towards these new goals?
- Are they in the S.M.A.R.T. format? If not, write them down using the S.M.A.R.T. goal-setting structure.
- How do you feel now about these new goals?

Goals are an important part of becoming self-made and achieving success. As you have no doubt realised while reading this book, it takes work, inner work and constant check-in and reflection to be able to live the life that you desire. You need to regularly check in with yourself to make sure how you are spending your days and how you are building your business aligns to your current values and vision for your life. It costs nothing to have a dream, so dream big.

14

Selling your product

The power of relationships

Helen Keller once said, 'Alone we can do so little; together we can do so much.' The first time I learned about the power of building positive relationships in business was when I worked in real estate in my early 20s. I discovered there are different styles of selling, and like anything, you need to learn the style that works best for you. It's also important to think about how your style will help you succeed in the long term.

As a real estate agent, you make money by selling property. In order to list more properties, you need to build a healthy database of sellers and buyers. According to the Australian Bureau of Statistics, the average Australian homeowner will sell their property every 11 years, so success in real estate is a long game. Now, admittedly, I didn't stay in real estate long enough to experience any real measure of success, like opening my own office, but it did teach me some valuable life lessons about the value and importance of relationship building in selling.

The opposite of relationship selling is *transactional selling*. It focuses on a one-off transaction, and there is no long-term relationship. I have worked in sales for over 20 years, and in my time, I have observed many great salespeople and some not-so-great salespeople. The ones who stood out were always more focused on the relationship and the long-term strategic opportunities that existed for both parties.

Sales is a skill that is more natural for some people than others, but you can and should definitely be training yourself on how to get better at sales, and constantly working on it. You may be wondering why we are discussing relationship selling if you run an ecommerce business. We'll get to that shortly. But, you are not just building a business behind a computer screen. In order to grow your brand, you are going to have to build and form relationships with many different people along your journey. In this chapter, I want to focus on one of the most important elements of selling: relationships and connection. While a connection can be a single touchpoint or, hopefully, the precursor to something more enduring, a relationship needs to be built up over time.

Building positive and mutually rewarding relationships in business is another critical foundation for becoming self-made and successful in business.

It's through building and nurturing relationships that you can grow and scale your business as well as collaborate with others. This takes time and effort, and there are some really important elements to master, such as kindness, authenticity, empathy, listening, responding, appreciation, respect, patience, gratitude and giving.

One of my greatest superpowers is relationship building and connecting with people. I love people, and I love to develop very deep and meaningful connections with others. Learning to do this has created many opportunities for my business over the past eight years.

Now, let's dive deeper into some really fundamental skills when it comes to building relationships and nurturing connections with people you meet on your journey.

Building lasting connections through relationship selling

Relationship selling is essentially where you, the salesperson, take the time to get to know your customer on a personal level, and then you develop a relationship based on shared interests, values and experiences.

I prefer to build personal relationships as this allows me to think more strategically about how to deliver something of value to my customers. The stronger your relationship with your customer, the deeper the partnership can go. I'm not sure who coined the saying, 'you should never mix business with pleasure', as some of the most pleasurable experiences I have ever had have been with my customers. The more you are able to focus on building a relationship with your customers—by getting to know them on a personal level, what shared interests you may have and what their values are—the more trust and rapport you will develop together.

One of your roles as a salesperson or business owner is to help your customers achieve success, whatever that looks like for them.

The more you are able to achieve this level of service, the better your chances are for repeat business, referrals and increased sales. The cherry on top: friendships can be formed. One of my soul sisters today started as a business partner of Shhh Silk. The friendships you are able to form by developing genuine, authentic relationships with your customers can be lifelong, and the benefits of those friendships can outweigh those of your original business together.

Now, building such deep, strong, personal relationships may not be appropriate in all sales situations, so you need to use your common sense. A strategic relationship with your customer may be more appropriate. Even though you may not be building a friendship, you still need to include all of the elements I mentioned previously, as this level of service and sales mastery will take your professional relationship with your customers and business partnerships further.

Many clients have shared with me over the years that they just don't know how to sell, or they don't have the confidence to sell.

Selling is a fear for some people. If this is you, then I definitely encourage you to re-read the exercises in Chapter 9 around mindset. You can overcome this fear with support, training, mentoring and practice.

I could write a whole book on the importance of mastering sales; however, you can read some books that have already been written on the subject, such as *The Psychology of Selling* by Brian Tracy. This book covers a range of selling techniques, including the different styles of selling, and offers practical advice on how to succeed in sales.

I think it's important not to see sales as a monetary outcome or a transaction, as that takes away all of the joy that is the magic of sales. Selling to me is about creating a shared experience for you, the customer, and perhaps their customers. It's about creating magic. Now what that magic looks like is completely up to you. The more special and customised you can make the process, the more successful you will find your experience, and the more you will begin to love the process of sales.

I'm going to share a story so you understand how I approach sales for Shhh Silk. Now, granted, I am very big on personal relationships when it comes to sales, so this may be too much for you initially, but you might find elements you can apply to your own business.

LIFE LESSON 15

Shhh Silk x The Beverly Hills Hotel collaboration

In January 2017, just 14 months after launching Shhh Silk, I travelled to the US with my two children for a short work trip and a holiday. For the last few days of the trip, I booked us into the magical and world-renowned Beverly Hills Hotel. The moment I entered the front doors, I was in love! It's hard to explain the feeling this hotel exudes; it feels alive. (If you get the chance to visit Beverly Hills, I would highly recommend a visit.)

I was lounging by the pool, drinking champagne, and I had a strange vision. I turned and said to my daughter, 'I'm going to make silk robes for this hotel.' She's used to my wild ideas, and we had a conversation about how incredible the scenery of The Beverly Hills Hotel would look printed on silk. Now, I must clarify a few details: firstly, I had never stayed at the hotel before and had no connection with any of the staff; secondly, I am not a fashion designer and had never designed sleepwear before. But at that moment, that afternoon, I had a strong vision of designing a robe for the hotel.

Whenever I travel, I always pack extra product samples, as I am always open to the fact that opportunities can be presented at any moment, and it's important to be prepared.

So I went to the hotel's retail store and asked if I could chat with the manager. When I approached the staff of the store (as a guest) and I asked if I could speak to the manager about stocking my products there, the team member apologised and said the director, Kristy, was away that weekend. He handed me Kristy's business card and said I should email her some information. I was bummed.

About 30 minutes later, we were walking back to the hotel from the pool. As we approached the door, I saw a woman in a navy blue suit with dark brown hair. I turned and said to my kids, 'That's Kristy.' They both looked at me puzzled and said, 'Mum the man told you she wasn't here this weekend.' I said, 'Guys, trust me, that is Kristy!' As we neared the door, she stepped forward to open it for us, I took a step in and said nervously, 'Excuse me, are you Kristy?' She smiled and said, 'Yes ma'am, can I assist you?'

I couldn't believe it! I was literally shaking. I said, 'Oh my goodness, please wait here, I have something in my room I need to grab for you.' I told my children to wait for me and I raced to my room to grab two silk pillowcases. I returned to the spa counter where Kristy was waiting. I passed her the pillowcases and said, 'Please sleep on these tonight. If you love them, can we please meet tomorrow?' I think she was slightly taken aback by the interaction. I was so excited, she must have been able to sense my enthusiasm and she politely agreed to test them out. The following morning I sent Kristy an email and asked her how her sleep experience was on our silk, and this was the first email I ever received from Kristy (who has now become one of my closest soul sisters).

> **Date:** Saturday, 14 January 2017 at 11:28 am
>
> **To:** Olivia Carr <info@shhhsilk.com>
>
> **Subject:** RE: Silk Pillowcases
>
> Good morning Olivia,
>
> Thank you for your follow up, I slept very well and loved the feel of the silk pillowcase.
>
> Please let me know if you are available this afternoon between 1 pm and 3 pm.
>
> Wishing you well and looking forward to your reply.
>
> Kind regards,
>
> Kristy

Kristy and I met that day at 1 pm. We mostly shared stories about our life journeys. Kristy spoke about her time in San Francisco and then moving to Los Angeles, and I shared my journey as a mother and how and why I started Shhh Silk. Kristy asked me if it was possible to create a sleepwear collection not only for women and men, but for children too. I said yes.

Always say yes, and work out the how later.

> We had formed a connection in just one hour together, over our love of people, collaboration, ideas and creativity. I have been working with Kristy and The Beverly Hills Hotel since our first launch in 2017, and since then we have grown our partnership into three collections expanding into women's, men's and children's sleepwear, accessories and resort wear. I have travelled to China with Kristy and shown her how her collection is made from start to finish. She has visited me in Australia and, recently, we both hiked in Joshua Tree together. We are going to be lifelong friends and business partners for years to come.

This example highlights one of the key lessons when it comes to relationships and sales. As Zig Ziglar shared, 'People don't buy for logical reasons; they buy for emotional reasons.' Relationships are built upon connection and trust. I have been blessed to be able to continue building my professional and personal relationship with Kristy since that first meeting over six years ago.

The other important factor with selling is you also need to stand out, take risks and be different. Kristy later shared with me that she receives hundreds of requests from brands across the globe wanting to collaborate with the hotel, but she only works with partners who are authentic and have a founder story to share beyond the product they are selling. You can revisit how to write your brand story in Chapter 4.

Grab out your notebook and pen, and let's work through your founder story and who you would love to collaborate with.

ACTIVITY

Your founder story

Your story

Write the answers to these questions.

- Why did you start your business?
- What is the story behind your brand?
- What is your story as the founder?
- How do you communicate these stories to others?
- Do you share these stories publicly?
- How could you share these stories?

Collaborations

Write a list of your dream partnerships or collaborations and answer the following questions.

- Why do you want to collaborate with them?
- What could the collaboration look like?
- What steps can you take now to work towards forming these collaborations?
- What steps will you take this week?

15

Harnessing influence

The power of PR and celebrity gifting

In the words of Oprah Winfrey, 'One of the biggest lessons I've learned is that celebrities are human beings. They're just people like you and me who happen to be famous, and they have the same flaws and insecurities as everyone else.'

I really want to break PR down as much as I can for you, as I still think there is some uncertainty around what exactly PR is. Most women I mentor think of PR as working with a PR agency and getting your brand published in articles. And yes, while this is one form of PR, it is only one form. Most PR (if not all) can be handled by you or your team. I am hugely passionate about PR. I went to university when I was 30 to study it. (Side lesson, if you didn't finish high school or get the end score you wanted, there are other pathways later in life.)

Let's start by looking at some of the different forms of marketing and PR. You may find you've already been doing some of these types of PR or marketing for your brand.

Media relations

This is a key aspect of PR that involves building and maintaining relationships with journalists, reporters and other members of the media. Your goal with media relations is to generate positive publicity and coverage for your business to build your profile. You do this by providing journalists or editors with newsworthy stories, expert commentary and other content that will be of interest to their audiences. This may involve creating press releases, arranging interviews and media appearances, providing background information and fact-checking, and responding to media inquiries and requests for information.

Social media

By using social media platforms, you can engage and entertain your audience and inform them about your brand. By engaging with comments, you can create relationships with your community. You can use social media for giveaways, polls, live sessions, behind-the-scenes content and more to create engagement and customer loyalty. It is important to create a social media content plan for your business, and there are many resources you can find online. The key is to find a good balance between informing, entertaining and engaging your audience.

Influencer marketing

This marketing strategy involves partnering with individuals (influencers) who have an engaged following on social media to promote your products and brand. The goal of your influencer marketing strategy is to leverage the influencer's reach and influence to promote your products to their audience in an authentic and engaging way. Influencers may specialise in specific niches, such as beauty, fitness, travel or food. You can partner with influencers through sponsored posts, product placements, brand collaborations and other forms of content creation in exchange for compensation or other incentives. Effective influencer marketing can help to increase your brand awareness, drive sales and build brand loyalty among a target audience.

Celebrity gifting

This form of PR involves gifting celebrities who align with your brand's values and mission with your products. It's important to be mindful of who you choose to gift to, and ensure that your product would be something of interest to them so as not to create more unnecessary waste in the ecommerce ecosystem. Save your inventory for celebrities who would genuinely enjoy using your product.

Content marketing

This marketing strategy involves creating and sharing valuable, relevant and consistent content to attract and retain your audience. An example of this could be a beauty brand creating a YouTube channel with makeup tutorials, skincare routines and product reviews that their target audience would find helpful.

Sponsorship

If you want to leverage sponsorship as a marketing strategy, you might sponsor or host events to promote your brand and your products. This could be a financial contribution that gets your brand listed on promotional materials, signage, digital coverage for the event, or it could involve donation of products to be used at the event, perhaps as a giveaway or prize. The goal is to increase your brand awareness and drive customer engagement.

The most successful form of PR and marketing for Shhh Silk has been celebrity gifting. Let me share the story about Shhh Silk's connection to the Kardashian family.

Shhh Silk x Kim Kardashian app giveaway

When I decided to start Shhh Silk in 2015, I had a very clear vision of Kim Kardashian using one of our silk pillowcases. I have watched and loved their TV series since it began, and one of Kim's grandmother's beauty tips was to always sleep on a silk pillowcase.

Around the same time there was a photo of Kim travelling while holding a black silk pillowcase that looked too large for her pillow, and I just believed I would be able to offer her a better quality and nicer fitting silk pillowcase than the one she currently owned. I had a goal (with action steps) to get my silk pillowcases delivered to Kim for her and her sisters to enjoy.

I shared in Chapter 3 how I flew to Los Angeles and hand delivered a box of silk pillowcases and a handwritten note to Kris Jenner. I offered to make them more silk pillowcases if they liked them. Several months later, Shhh Silk gifted silk pillowcases to guests at a PR event, and Kim's stylist at the time happened to be there and received one of our silk pillowcases. A few days later I received an email from our US-based PR company letting us know that Kim's team had requested some silk pillowcases, and had also invited Shhh Silk to be involved in a giveaway for her followers on her web and mobile app.

To this day, I don't really know why Kim decided to be so generous and allow Shhh Silk to be part of such incredible unpaid and organic opportunities with her app—and we did more than one. However, what I do know is just how incredibly grateful I am and always will be for her love and support.

From the very first touchpoint I had with the Kardashian family back in 2016, I have always aimed to be kind, genuine, authentic, vulnerable, giving, grateful and, above all else, thoughtful. I have sent celebration gifts for so many of the family's milestones, from the launching of their businesses, their birthdays and even the birth of their children.

As a founder and as the brand owner, I have always valued relationships over outcomes. A lesson I learnt in my earlier years working as a real estate agent was that *genuine relationships can be lifelong, and transactions are one-off.*

At 11:11 (thank you, universe) on 8 December 2016, I received an email from Kim's executive assistant. Prior to this email, all of the communication I had received had come via my PR team from their editorial or PR team. In the email Kim's EA told me that Kim loved the pillowcases and asked whether it would be possible to send a few more. I was thrilled!

It would also later become the introduction to some other beautiful souls that work for the family or their brands that I am still connected to today. I believe in connecting with people, not status. I enjoyed many DMs and email chats with Kim's EA and we even shared a night out together for dinner when I was in LA. I've sent gifts and products to many of the family's team members as I am eternally grateful for their generosity, support and love. Nothing each of the team members has ever done for me or Shhh Silk has gone unappreciated or unnoticed. I am forever grateful.

One communication I received that really touched me was a handwritten card from Khloé giving thanks for custom pillow slips I'd sent. It is something I cherish and protect, as it signifies our connection and mutual respect for each other.

If you are going to gift celebrities with your products, it is so important that you build genuine relationships with their teams. It never feels nice when you experience one-sided relationships with friends, so it's important you are not building one-sided relationships with a celebrity's team. Kindness and generosity will take you far.

The most important element of gifting I believe is the first impression you leave on the person receiving the gift. Let me share an example of one of the gifts we sent to Kylie Jenner and why she chose to share it on her Snapchat.

Creative gifting ideas and Kylie Jenner

On 10 August 2017, Kylie Jenner turned 20. Ten days prior she had launched her Kylie Cosmetics birthday bundle, which was a giant pink box of beauty products. The moment the birthday bundle was released, the team and I got to work planning a birthday gift for Kylie that would feel personal and customised so she could enjoy it while celebrating her birthday and the huge success of her launch. We started by researching the colours she had chosen for her new birthday bundle, and we decided to colour match our gift to it. We organised (very quickly) to get some of our pink Shhh Silk sleep masks monogrammed for Kylie and her squad (a name used to refer to a close group of people who hang out together).

Gifting celebrities and influential people is all about detail and thought. We used Kylie's font for her sleep mask so it would feel more on-brand to her. We knew sending our product on its own was not going to have the impact we were hoping, so we reached out to a local Melbourne woman who was just starting her own custom cookie company, and asked if she could very quickly bake some cookies in the custom colours and some Shhh Silk–branded cookies to accompany them. She worked her magic and we express shipped the birthday box off to Kylie's assistant (figure 15.1 is a sneak peek at the gift we sent).

Figure 15.1 Kylie's Shhh Silk birthday gift

This wasn't the first time we'd gifted Kylie products, however, it was the first time Kylie shared our product. She shared a selfie of herself and all of her squad wearing our pink Shhh Silk sleep masks. Our pink silk sleep masks have been a constant sell-out ever since!

Monogramming silk sleep masks does have a big impact for branding, but it is not practical and not something Kylie could have slept in as the embroidery goes through both sides of the silk. This doesn't make them a soft sleep experience. We have since updated our processes to vinyl press on the front side only. Always obsess over the customer (or in this case, the celebrity) experience.

It's the experience, not the gesture

When it comes to gifting celebrities, high-profile individuals or influencers who align with your brand, it is important to consider what the moment will be like for the recipient. I'm a strong believer that small brands wanting to gift celebrities need to focus more on the experience they are providing them rather than the product they are wanting to gift them. Eight times out of ten, when Shhh Silk gifts celebrities, it is not even our product that we are gifting. Or, at the very least, it is not just our product. If you are a small brand like Shhh Silk, you likely don't have a large enough marketing budget to do sponsorship deals with celebrities, so you need to spend time and energy on creating amazing experiences and moments. It's truly the simple, thoughtful acts that go a long way.

Another simple yet thoughtful gifting moment was when I sent Kim Kardashian the largest box of Nerds that exists in the United States. What do nerds have to do with Shhh Silk? Nothing. They have absolutely nothing to do with Shhh Silk pillowcases. However, they are one of Kim Kardashian's favourite sweets. So when I heard Kim talking on social media about this flavour being her favourite Nerds combination, I did what comes naturally to me: I connected. I set about creating an unexpected moment for Kim that she would enjoy. I immediately found the world's biggest box of Nerds on Amazon and shipped them straight to Kim.

Why would I send Nerds when they have nothing to do with my brand? I sent the Nerds to Kim Kardashian because it wasn't about me or Shhh Silk. It wasn't about getting our silk products shared on Kim's social media accounts. This moment was about the connection I have built with Kim, and the feeling I knew this random act of kindness would give her.

Connection and feeling connected—truly connected—is a basic human need.

The lesson here is not about silk pillowcases, your product or Nerds. The lesson is about the importance of building, maintaining and respecting genuine connections and relationships with others. Relationships are not about you; they are not about your brand, service offering or your product; and they are definitely not transactional. The next time you think of shipping your new, amazing product to a celebrity, influencer or high-profile person: stop. Stop and ask yourself: is this parcel all about me and my brand? How can I make this more about the person receiving this parcel and what they love, more than my own wants? How can I truly connect with this person? *This is where the real magic lies.*

It's time to grab your notebook and pen. Let's start with a list of people you'd love to experience your brand.

ACTIVITY

Creating a celebrity gift plan

- Write a list of ten people you would love to experience your product.
- Now write a list of all of the people these people associate with. Who is in their squad?
- Starting with the first person on your list, ask yourself, what do they love? What are their favourite flowers or colours, when is their birthday, what other special individual likes does this person have? (For example, Kendall Jenner loves horses; her birthday is 3 November; she is a Scorpio; she loves mindfulness, sound bowls, her home; and she has her own tequila label. Some of the people in her squad are Jen Atkin, Mary Phillips and Dani Michelle.)
- What is a moment or a random act of kindness you can create that this person would genuinely enjoy?
- If you can't ship to this person directly, can you ship it to their work address, or can you send something to a member of their team or their squad?
- Repeat this exercise for everyone on your list. Make a plan to create customised, truly personal moments. Write down what you need to do, or what you need to purchase to create them.

It's key to remember that these gifting moments are not one-off moments. They are the start of a long and meaningful connection between you and the recipient. Celebrities have access to everything these days, so you are not providing them with products they don't want or need (this just adds to landfill and waste). You are creating moments and experiences to make these people feel something special and meaningful in that moment. Random acts of kindness can evoke a range of different feelings and emotions for both the giver and the receiver. For the receiver, it can create feelings of gratitude, appreciation and happiness. These emotions are priceless and cannot be bought; they can only be experienced. *You are creating experiences for people.*

16

Adapting to change

Navigating uncertainty in business and life

It's time to explore one of my favourite aspects of business, and that is overcoming adversity, setbacks and hardship. Over time, it has become a favourite topic of mine because it's something that I've had to revisit time and time again, and every time, it's through this process that I have achieved the most personal and professional growth. If you are building a business, you will resonate deeply with this chapter. No one in business is immune to uncertainty, setbacks or hardship. It's part of life and business. So there is no point trying to avoid it; all you can do is accept it is part of the journey. Stress-reduction expert Jon Kabat-Zinn advises, 'You can't stop the waves, but you can learn to surf.'

My therapist reminds me often that the only certainty in life is uncertainty. And the same goes for running a business. You will experience many hurdles over the course of building, growing and scaling your business, such as inventory or stock issues, new brands entering your space, disruptions to supply chains, cash flow challenges, human resource challenges, system-related challenges, economic downturns, mindset and so many others. It's important to remember this as you continue on your journey: the bigger the business, often means the bigger the issues.

It is inevitable that, over the life of your business, you will face economic downturns that will have a direct effect on your revenue. When economic conditions are harsh, consumer demand slows, and spending decreases in some sectors, and retail is one of them.

Ultimately, what moments like this mean for you as a business owner, is that you need to be ready to surf big waves. Learning to surf in business is how you survive. But learning to surf also means there will be times you feel like you are drowning. Sometimes you will experience the excitement of riding the waves and other times you will get knocked down. The lesson in this chapter is understanding there are always ups and downs. So strap yourself in for the ride of your life!

I'm going to share some of the ways in which I have learnt to surf in my business over the past eight years.

Being adaptable to change

While running Shhh Silk, I have had to learn to become faster and more in tune with what I need to change or innovate in order to continue growing the profitability of the business. For the first few years, I didn't have my finger on the pulse when it came to the cash position and understanding essential financial terms, such as the run rate. (The run rate is how much cash you have left in your business to keep you afloat if your cash flow suddenly dried up. How long that cash lasts determines how long your business can keep operating with no money coming in.)

When COVID hit Australia, consumer spending behaviour changed almost overnight. I remember our first ever three consecutive donut days of no sales on our online store. It was only a matter of days before our business bank account rolled into the negative, and it felt as though the moment I had been dreading since first starting Shhh Silk was here. I was seriously facing the closure of the business. I quickly realised that I had a very short cash flow run rate, and including outstanding invoices, I estimated we would have enough money coming in to pay the team for a maximum of six weeks. If nothing changed, we would have to close the business by May 2020.

So what did I do, and how did I deal with the harsh reality of closing Shhh Silk?

I shared on social media and LinkedIn the severity of the impact of the pandemic on our business, along with a screenshot of our negative balance bank account. I opened myself up completely. I had nothing to hide, nothing more to lose, and I decided I could only gain by sharing my truth. So that's what I did. I reached out to my wholesale customers, our online community and our loyal customer base that we had nurtured for six years and asked for their support. I shared the reality of our situation and created a social campaign called #saveourstaff.

This was (unbeknownst to me at the time) a huge turning point for me in choosing to speak as a leader in the business space. This was when I started operating the business from a space of values, not ego. The response, love and support from our community reshaped my openness to sharing the realities of owning a small business, both the highs and the lows. This is why I am now an advocate for sharing more truth about both the struggles and triumphs of running a business. It's also why I decided to write this book: so I could share what it feels like to run a small business. Sometimes it's downright terrifying.

But reaching out to our customers was just the beginning. I knew that we needed to make significant changes to our operations and product offerings if we were going to survive the pandemic.

I started by looking at our existing products and identifying areas where we could cut costs without sacrificing quality. I streamlined our inventory and focused on selling our most profitable and popular items (a practice we still do today). I also shifted our business model to offer comfort products by other brands, such as bath salts, books, candles, heat packs, crystals and more. This also supported other small female business owners, as we could order from them and show them support while offering our customers new products. At the same time, I began to research new product categories. I knew that we needed to diversify our offerings to ensure that we had multiple revenue streams.

Practicing self-care to manage stress and anxiety

Having experienced burnout in business before, it was important for me to be mindful of the impact that this challenging period could have on my mental health and, in particular, my anxiety. I made sure to get outside daily and go walking along the beach or in park and surround myself with nature. Over the years, I have discovered the significant impact being around nature has on my mental state. When you find yourself in one of those moments where things in your business feel too hard, or you can't see a way through, I encourage you to take time away from your business and spend some time in nature. If you're curious to understand more about the benefits of nature therapy (also known as eco-therapy), make a note in your notebook to research the benefits of this later.

I started reading more self-development books, listening to manifesting abundance meditations and made sure to dial down the media noise and instead fill my mind with positive content, so as not to feel defeated by the world event that was taking place around me. I dialled down the noise and created new stories for myself that were positive and uplifting.

When things feel tough, it's natural to think you need to work longer and harder; however, this can create more feelings of stress and overwhelm or even lead to burnout.

It is during the more challenging periods of running a business that you need to take a step back and try to seek some clarity on what is happening around you. It's far easier to work through challenges when you are not overwhelmed or stressed.

This is also an important time to go inwards and focus on your own self-care and self-development. Surround yourself with positive people, listen to inspiring business or mindset podcasts, read motivational books, seek out a self-development course or start therapy with a psychologist. Trying to survive the challenging moments alone is not the best option for your business or your health, and you never need to go it alone.

If you are currently working alone, it's especially important to seek support during difficult times in your business. Beyond Blue offers an incredible free program to assist business owners who are experiencing a tough time. It's called 'NewAccess for Small Business Owners' and it is a guided self-help mental health coaching program. It's free, confidential and convenient. I have included the link in the resources at the end of this book.

It can often feel like you shouldn't be taking time away from work to focus on yourself and your mental wellbeing when things are tough; however, the sooner you can introduce daily practices into your routine to support your overall mental, physical and emotional needs, the easier you will find it to deal with adversity and setbacks. The size of the problem you're dealing with will begin to feel more manageable the more balanced you feel as an individual.

If you're looking for some strategies to better manage feelings of stress and anxiety, revisit some of the mental health toolkit techniques we covered in Chapter 8.

Developing a growth mindset

I discovered the power of having a growth mindset from a book called *Mindset: The new psychology of success* by Carol Dweck, who is a professor of psychology at Stanford University.

We discussed the importance of a growth mindset in Chapter 9. Learning to have a growth mindset will allow you to see challenges and failures as opportunities for growth and learning, rather than as setbacks or indications of your own limitations. It allows you to embrace new experiences, take risks, and seek feedback to improve yourself.

It can be incredibly difficult to maintain or develop a growth or abundance mindset when you are struggling financially or feel as though the business is not growing at the speed you would like. It feels extremely counterintuitive to operate from a growth mindset; however, it is much easier to be creative, problem-solve and think of new opportunities when you have a positive mindset.

An example of how having a growth mindset has helped me survive in business was when I took a risk by introducing silk face coverings into our business at the start of the pandemic. This ultimately turned the financial position of the business around in a matter of months, and resulted in our biggest single sales year ever.

Along with maintaining a positive, growth mindset, I went back to some techniques I had learnt earlier on in my business journey around design thinking and mind mapping, and started to think of new ideas, solutions, products, cost savings and so on to survive this challenging time in business.

Design thinking means taking a problem-solving approach that involves understanding and empathising with your customer, defining their problem, creating possible solutions, prototyping those solutions and testing them. It is a creative and iterative process that helps you to come up with innovative solutions that meet customers' needs.

I also started mind mapping ideas and solutions that started with a central idea and then branched out to related ideas and subcategories.

This can be a powerful tool in ecommerce to drive sales. If you are currently feeling as though you are stuck for ideas to generate more profit in your business, try this technique.

This is a simple exercise you can do to create ideas for your business.

ACTIVITY

Mind mapping your business

You'll need at least three team members for this activity (the more brains thinking of new ideas, the better). If you don't have a team, invite some friends or family over for dinner and ask them to join you in this process.

Have a bunch of sticky notes and pens and a timer.

Come up with a general theme for what you want to explore, such as new categories or product expansion.

Set the timer for 30 minutes and invite everyone to write down as many ideas as they can think of during this time on sticky notes. Remind everyone that no idea is a bad idea. It's important to encourage unrestricted thinking at this early stage, so don't come up with reasons why it wouldn't work as you'll dismiss potentially winning ideas. This is a brain dump of as many new ideas as you can capture during your allocated timeframe.

When the timer ends, share your ideas with the group. Discard any duplicates.

Categorise the ideas into similar topics. This can be anything that makes sense for the theme you are working on. So for Shhh Silk, all items related to sleep could be clustered together, and all items related to beauty could be clustered together.

Get a large whiteboard or pinboard and set up your sprint board. A sprint board is a visual management project planning tool used to track the progress of a project or initiative. It's typically a physical board or wall that is divided into columns that represent different stages of the project or design process. For example, a common sprint board layout might have columns for 'to do', 'doing' and 'done' or 'on track', 'off track with a plan' or 'off track'.

The next step is for you to identify any ideas that are not relevant right now or don't fit your theme. Place them on the bottom of your sprint board in an area called 'for later', or we like to use 'parking lot'. You may decide to give them their own sprint boards later.

Now it's time for you to break every sticky note you have into all the different tasks needed to achieve these goals. This might mean one sticky note idea ends up having several small tasks and several sticky notes. On the sticky notes, write: *who* (who is responsible for the task), *by when* (when will this task be completed) and *how long* (how long this task will take).

Now it's time to place all of the sticky notes (individual tasks) in the relevant column on your sprint board. Do this by working out how many weeks this goal will take, and then place the sticky notes on the board in order of the week they are due. It's important to make sure that, if you only want to work 10 hours a week or your team only works 10 hours a week, that the amount of time allocated to complete these tasks (plus their or your other work) is realistic. For example, if your warehouse packer only works 10 hours a week packing orders, you may only be able to allocate one or two hours of new tasks a week to allow them to complete their usual work of packing orders. If you have allocated too many tasks for one week, move some of the sticky notes to weeks where you have fewer tasks.

From here, it's time to kick the projects off. If you have a team, I suggest having weekly sprint board catch ups to discuss what was completed that week and what's on track, off track with a plan, or off track. You can then discuss why it's off track and what needs to be done to bring it back on track. During your catch up, move the sticky notes to their relevant week or column on the board.

This process can be extremely helpful when running a business as it allows you to problem-solve, innovate and develop creative ideas, and break goals or tasks down into manageable, bite-sized pieces. It allows you to stay on track by taking daily action, which you now (after reading Chapter 10) understand is your secret weapon to becoming self-made.

How Shhh Silk used the sprint board task to generate a profit

One of the game-changing ideas that came from this process was deciding to create silk face coverings very early on in the pandemic, well before they were mandated in Australia. After a brainstorm, one sticky note read: *Research this idea: are any countries wearing masks*? I became aware that some states in the USA were mandating the use of face coverings, and while at that time I didn't know if this would be the case in Australia, I decided to take a risk and turn all of the spare silk fabric we had in our factories into silk face coverings. We then created an entire sprint board to launch silk face masks globally.

We reached out to Adore Beauty saying we believed these products would likely become a necessity, and asked if they would introduce them to their online customer base. Adore Beauty became an early adopter of our silk face masks, and by the time the masks landed in Australia, they were all sold out (on pre-order), and we were placing orders weekly from that moment on for over 12 months. If we hadn't stopped and used the sprint board, we would likely never have thought about introducing the one product that ended up saving our business and skyrocketing us into our biggest profit-generating year.

Having a growth mindset, especially when times are tough, can help you view challenges as opportunities for growth and learning, embrace new experiences, take calculated risks and seek feedback to improve yourself. To survive challenging times, it's important to use techniques, such as design thinking and mind mapping, to come up with new ideas, solutions and cost savings. Adversity builds character, these are the times you *must* dig deep.

While, initially, hardship, setbacks and adversity feel challenging and overwhelming, in my experience, once you've found balance internally again and survived the wave, you often come out the other side feeling excited and having experienced something completely different than you were expecting. With this new strength and confidence, you'll know that, if you survived this wave, you can also survive the next one.

I want to use this moment to thank our loyal customers who helped us keep our doors open long enough to stay on the wave. It was their support that allowed us to keep going and they supported the risk we took in investing in a new product category. They are the reason Shhh Silk still exists. Together, we get to do good and make an impact.

While the pandemic was an unpredictable event that no one saw coming, this is a reminder to not give up, even in situations that seem out of your control. A growth mindset can lead you to unexpected success and growth.

Important reminder

At no point, though, should you sacrifice your own mental health in order to overcome external factors out of your control. I was very prepared mentally for the possibility that Shhh Silk may not survive the pandemic, and while I found a winning product that ended up being our lifeline, this was not the case for many other small businesses. Never feel you have failed if you need to close your business. If you have tried everything you can, and there are external factors at play, like a pandemic, then closing your business is just the reality of the situation.

You are not your business. You are not responsible for every outcome of your business. This is another important lesson I have learnt since stepping out of my ego. Your health and mental wellbeing should be your first priority at all times on your business journey. Yes, you will feel challenged often; yes, you will be tired and get run down; yes, running your business will be one of the hardest things you have ever done; and yes, you will have to make sacrifices—but know your limit. And know that it's okay to do what is best for you, above anything or anyone else.

17

Reclaiming your freedom

Remembering the purpose of your business beyond stress and overwork

As I sit in the morning sun on the alfresco deck at Victoria's at Wategos in Byron Bay, I'm staring at the picturesque backdrop of palm trees, birds of paradise and clear blue skies. The smell of sunscreen is in the air and the sound of the water fountains gurgle away. I am suddenly reminded again why I started Shhh Silk all those years ago.

It was never really about making $50 000 000 or sailing off into the sunset, which are some of the empty goals I believed were a measure of success back in 2015. At the time, my ego believed that if I achieved these things, it meant I had made it—there was no greater success (or so I thought).

Admittedly, when starting a business, it's easy to think you need to set a monetary goal for success. That number will be different for everyone, but for me, it was $50 000 000. I don't know where that number came from; it could have been from a millionaire mindset course I attended, or it could have been a number I just plucked out of my head that sounded big enough and scary enough to drive me to aim higher than I believed possible at that moment.

I am not suggesting that having monetary goals in business is a negative thing. You need some measures in place to be able to grow your business and track your progress. But I really believed it was the dollar amount that the business would generate that would end up being my personal measure of success as a founder. That achieving that is what would make me self-made and able to live the life I desired for myself.

Thankfully, this is just not the case. Shhh Silk has sold more than $10 000 000 in silk sleepwear, pillowcases and accessories, and while this is just 20 per cent of my original monetary goal, I have realised that it is not the money generated from your business that is important—it's the *freedom exchange* for your time, resources, energy and money that is really important. This is the ultimate measure of true success, and that is what will allow you to live a self-made life.

So long as you focus on building a profitable business that allows you time, as much as it does financial freedom, you are going to feel far more successful than someone who gets so caught up in the day-to-day operations and the demands of running a business that they experience stress, overwork and burnout.

Taking mini vacations on your own, with loved ones, family or friends regularly to fill up your cup, rest and rejuvenate is how you are going to continue to build a healthy business. These pleasurable moments will be the fuel that continues to ignite the fire within you to keep going and growing your business. The more freedom and time you build and allow for yourself, the more rewarding your business journey will become. You will start to have more creativity and mental space for new ideas within your business, and a new sense of passion and motivation to drive the business forward (who knows, even potentially hitting your original monetary goal) from a place of newfound meaning and purpose.

The freedom to choose

Let's talk about time. Time is a non-renewable resource that, once used, cannot be replaced or regained. No matter your wealth or status, we each only get 24 hours in a day. You can never buy more time.

While it is important to set goals, to keep growing and to stretch yourself out of your comfort zone, it is equally important to stay present in the moment and enjoy the time you have today.

I truly believe that you do not need to have a multi-million-dollar business to be self-made. If you are earning enough money to support the lifestyle you desire to live a big and meaningful life, then you already have a successful business.

While I reference balance and freedom a lot, I do want to acknowledge that this reward for effort takes time and work. If I hadn't put in all of the effort and work (both external and internal) required in the past few years to turn the financial position of Shhh Silk around, then I would not be in the position I am today to enjoy more balance and freedom. This daily effort and work has seen me achieve incredible things in my life, from raising my children, to climbing out of debt, to building my career, to growing a global business, to purchasing property on my own, to travelling the world, to mentoring women, to writing this book and to finally being able to enjoy more freedom in my life. I have a very big life. I am proud of myself for the way in which I have chosen to live my life. I am proud of my ability to learn from mistakes and not allow them to derail me from living a bigger life.

You have everything it takes to build your ideal life. Remove any unnecessary time pressure you have placed on yourself to get there, remove any financial measures you may have placed on yourself that you thought would define you as successful.

Ask yourself these questions:

- What does being self-made mean to you?
- What is your true definition of success?

And now take those answers and make that your new vision for your self-made life. Let that drive you and your business forward. Let that motivate you.

You define your own success

At the end of the day, the flashy cars, the super yachts, the designer clothing and the handbags are all just status symbols and not a true measure of success on their own.

The woman on the Byron Bay beach on a sunny afternoon, watching the surfers ride the waves while enjoying time with her girlfriends, long evening chats, nourishing food and belly laughs is a different picture of a self-made woman. This week that woman is me. I chose to share some of my success with three friends, and treat them to a weekend away in Byron Bay to nourish our souls, discover more about ourselves and strengthen our connection. Being able to choose how I spend my time and who I spend it with is my new barometer for success.

When I reflect back to my true core purpose and values, it was always about freedom and time. The simple freedom to be able to pick up my son from school each afternoon, something I still cherish all these years later. Having the time to attend events or family moments I would otherwise miss when I was working in the corporate world. To be able to travel any time of the year, to anywhere in the world, and for longer than the allotted four weeks a year you are given as an employee.

It took me about six years to realise I needed to change the way I was thinking about success and running my business. The story I had been telling myself was that other founders would think I never worked or didn't work hard enough if I was seen walking along the beach every morning or attending a lunchtime gym session. I felt guilty when I started work when I *felt* like starting work, and didn't buy in to the idea that the more successful you are, the longer and harder you should be working. None of this feels true to me anymore, nor does it align to my values of what being self-made is.

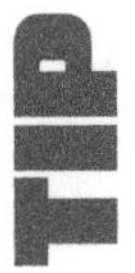

The more time I can spend doing the things that I love, and focusing on my overall health and wellbeing, the more successful I feel and become.

Success is completely subjective and should only be measured on an individual basis based on an individual's own values. The Oxford dictionary describes success as 'the accomplishment of an aim or purpose'.

As humans, we all have our own purpose. That's why it's okay for people to sail around on their super yachts, or showcase their latest designer purchases on Instagram, as these are personal measures of success to the individual sharing them. They align to their values in that moment. Your success will look vastly different to others, and that is a beautiful thing. That means you have worked out how to live in alignment with your values and your purpose.

Enjoy your success, and don't feel the need to compare your successful life to someone online who you may not have ever met in person. We are all on our own self-discovery journey, and while you may be watching someone online sharing their newest Chanel haul or driving their custom G-Wagon, and wondering what you're doing wrong as you aren't *there* yet, that person could very well be an old version of me. A person who used to share designer items online as a mask for the unfulfilling life I was living and the unresolved healing work I needed to do.

Please remember: 'comparison is the thief of joy'. If you desire a Chanel bag in the future (or something similar), then set yourself a goal to buy yourself the bag. But make sure it's because you love the bag, not to impress strangers on the internet, and definitely not because you think the bag validates your self-worth—it doesn't.

You, your soul and your essence validate your worth. But I get it. I love a nice LV moment now and then, I can be bougie at times (so I've been told by one of my best friends, Jarrad), but because I enjoy these things for me and not for strangers on the internet, I feel good about it.

I want to invite you to do an exercise now about designing your dream life. With everything you have learnt and reflected on while reading this book, it's time to really get honest with yourself about what your self-made life looks like. If your dream life includes super yachts, a pimped-out G-Wagon and attaining more material things, there is absolutely no judgement here. Gosh, my dream car is a black Bentley. Your version of self-made is just that—your version. So long as living the life that you design doesn't lead you down a path of burnout, comparison and overwhelm, or make you feel as though you have gone too far off the path of your innermost values, then you should absolutely start building this life for yourself.

ACTIVITY

Designing your self-made life

Let's start designing your self-made life. Grab your notebook and pen. Write the following at the top of the page:

My self-made life looks like:

Now, write down all of the things that your self-made life includes, such as a house, investment, holidays, experiences, material things and so on. Really get clear on what you see in your self-made life.

My self-made life feels like:

How do you want to feel each day as you start to build your self-made life? Examples can be feeling more gratitude, less overwhelmed, more energetic, lighter mentally, proud, healthy, inspired etc.

My self-made life aligns to my values by:

Write down how your self-made life aligns to your values. If your value is freedom, then perhaps your new self-made life allows you more time and space each day to do the things you love to do and spend time with the people you want to spend more quality time with.

What has stopped me in the past from building my self-made life:

Be honest with yourself about the circumstances, events, people, and limiting beliefs that may have prevented you from taking the daily steps to build out your self-made life, and make a list of all the solutions to overcome these obstacles.

Changes I will make from today to build my self-made life:

Think of some actions you can start/stop/continue doing to build out your dream self-made life. Perhaps it's something like starting to understand your personal money story and working on writing a new one.

Why this self-made life is important to me:

Really get clear about why building this next version of your big life is important for you. Do this in as much detail as possible. Use unrestricted and unlimited thinking when you are designing your dream self-made life.

There it is—your *very own* one-page roadmap to building your own big self-made life. Keep this on your bedside table and read it each night before bed and first thing in the morning before you touch your phone. If you feel comfortable and brave enough to share, I'd love to see your dream life plan. You can DM it to me over on Instagram at @self_madeacademy.

You can update and revise your self-made life plan as often as you like. And it's fine to aspire to want more for your life or less in some areas. Your dream self-made life is your life. No one else's.

In conclusion

In a world where we consume so much media and are constantly surrounded by comparisons about needing more, doing more and having more, it is so important to come back to yourself often and remind yourself what it is that is really important to you right now. How do you want to spend your days? Does the life you are living today fill you up? Does it align to your values? And, most importantly, does it feel meaningful to you and give you a sense of purpose? There is absolutely nothing wrong with desiring more financial wealth and financial freedom; it is something that I value deeply myself. However, what is most important is the *why* behind the self-made life you desire. Acquiring more wealth is only one part of living a meaningful and impactful self-made life.

My parting message for you is to not get caught up in believing that living a fulfilling and meaningful self-made life means that you have to push yourself to the point of burnout and not enjoy the present moment. Time is a finite resource; tomorrow is never guaranteed. Remember to live in the *now* as often as you can. Always be grateful for what you already have, and continue to strive to live each day with purpose. This is what makes you self-made.

With love and gratitude,

Olivia Carr xo

In conclusion

JOIN ME AT SELF-MADE ACADEMY

Your self-made journey doesn't end here. If you want to continue working on your self-made life and business, join us at Self-Made Academy, an online community serving female ecommerce startup and small business owners looking for support, connection, advice, tips, mentoring, training, workshops and community. The academy offers access to monthly expert-led masterclasses, where you'll learn from some of the most successful entrepreneurs and industry experts on topics such as marketing, finance, operations, mental health and wellbeing, and more.

I believe in taking a holistic approach to business, which is why our community also provides support and accountability to help you achieve your goals. You'll be able to engage daily with your peers and me, as your lead mentor, as well as other experts in the industry, to share ideas, troubleshoot problems, celebrate wins, connect and build your network. Our community is built on the principles of collaboration, accountability and growth.

I can't wait to welcome you to the Self-Made Academy!

www.self-madeacademy.com.au

Instagram: @self_madeacademy

MENTAL HEALTH RESOURCES

If you've just finished reading this book, then you already know how important taking care of your mental health is for all aspects of your life. Everyone struggles at points in their life, and help is available. A good support network is crucial, both for your personal and professional life, and a therapist can give you the tools and strategies to manage what you are feeling.

- Lifeline (13 11 14): If you're feeling as though you are in crisis, Lifeline is a free service that operates 24 hours a day. They also have a face to face and online service.
- Beyond Blue (beyondblue.org.au): This organisation has supports for people with anxiety, depression and suicidal ideation. They have a suite of resources and can connect you to a mental health professional.
- MyMirror (mymirror.com.au): I found this to be the fastest way for me to see a psychologist. There are wait times to see psychologists in some states, and this online option matches you with one of their experienced psychologists suited to your needs and schedule.
- This Way Up (thiswayup.org.au): This not-for-profit organisation helps people experiencing anxiety and depression.

For small business owners

- Beyond Blue NewAccess for Small Business Owners (beyondblue.org.au/get-support/newaccess-mental-health-coaching/newaccess-for-small-business-owners): This free 'guided self-help mental health coaching program' specifically targeting small business owners with fewer than 20 employees.

Chapter 1

1. Black Dog Institute n.d., 'Anxiety and depression during pregnancy and the postnatal period', Black Dog Institute, blackdoginstitute.org.au/wp-content/uploads/2022/06/Depression-during-preg nancy.pdf.

Chapter 2

2. Kay, MF 2016, 'Overcoming my money story', *Forbes*, forbes.com/sites/michaelkay/2016/12/06/overcoming-your-money-story/?sh=50d2 11e25bb2.

Chapter 3

3. Petty J 2005, 'Start me up', University of Technology Sydney, uts.edu.au/sites/default/files/Start_me_up.pdf.

Chapter 5

4. Voidonicolas V 2022, 'How much does it cost to start a business?' (Research), Shopify, shopify .com/au/blog/cost-to-start-business.
5. Macdonald M 2022, 'How to start an ecommerce business in 2023' (Practical guide), Shopify, shopify. com/au/blog/ecommerce-business-blueprint.

Chapter 7

6. English-Grammar-Lessons.com 2022, 'Children should be seen and not heard – meaning, origin and usage', English-Grammar-Lessons.com, english-grammar-lessons.com/children-should-be-seen-and-not-heard-meaning/.

Chapter 8

7. Waters S 2023, 'The ups and downs of a Type A personality', Better Up, betterup.com/blog/type-a-personality.
8. EveryMind n.d., 'Key facts', EveryMind, everymind.org.au/understanding-mental-health/mental-health/mental-health-key-facts.

Chapter 9

9. Smith J 2020, 'Growth mindset vs fixed mindset: How what you think affects what you achieve', Mindset Health, mindsethealth.com/matter/growth-vs-fixed-mindset.

Chapter 10

10. Haddon R 2020, 'How to practice self-acceptance (and why that's not the same as complacency)', MBG Mindfulness, mindbodygreen.com/articles/4-strategies-for-practicing-radical-self-acceptance.
11. Mind Tools n.d., 'Imposter syndrome', Mind Tools, mindtools.com/azio7m7/impostor-syndrome.

Chapter 13

12. Brown B n.d., 'Dare to lead list of values', Brené Brown, brenebrown.com/resources/dare-to-lead-list-of-values/.

13. Bard College n.d., 'Setting goals', Bard College, cce.bard.edu/files/Setting-Goals.pdf.